A TOAST

IF YOU'RE GOING TO LIE, LIE TO SAVE A FRIEND.

IF YOU'RE GOING TO CHEAT, CHEAT DEATH.

IF YOU'RE GOING TO STEAL, STEAL A PRETTY GIRL'S HEART.

AND IF YOU'RE GOING TO DRINK, DRINK WITH ME.

EST. MMXIII

Inspiring | Educating | Creating | Entertaining

Brimming with creative inspiration, how-to projects, and useful information to enrich your everyday life, Quarto Knows is a favorite destination for those pursuing their interests and passions. Visit our site and dig deeper with our books into your area of interest: Quarto Creates, Quarto Cooks, Quarto Homes, Quarto Lives, Quarto Drives, Quarto Explores, Quarto Gifts, or Quarto Kids.

First published in 2018 by Voyageur Press, an imprint of The Quarto Group, 401 Second Avenue North, Suite 310, Minneapolis, MN 55401 USA. Telephone: (612) 344-8100 Fax: (612) 344-8692

QuartoKnows.com

Voyageur Press titles are also available at discount for retail, wholesale, promotional, and bulk purchase. For details, contact the Special Sales Manager by email at specialsales@quarto.com or by mail at The Quarto Group, Attn: Special Sales Manager, 401 Second Avenue North, Suite 310, Minneapolis, MN 55401 USA.

Library of Congress Cataloging-in-Publication Data

Names: Volk, Andrew, 1983- author. | Volk, Briana, 1982- author.
Title: Northern hospitality with the Portland Hunt + Alpine Club : craft
    cocktails, Scandinavian food, Portland culture / Andrew Volk, Briana Volk.
Description: Minneapolis, Minnesota : Voyageur Press, 2018.
Identifiers: LCCN 2017057360 | ISBN 9780760357934 (hardback)
Subjects: LCSH: Cooking, Scandinavian. | Cooking--Maine--Portland. | Portland
    Hunt + Alpine Club (Portland, Maine) | BISAC: COOKING / Regional & Ethnic
    / American / New England. | COOKING / Beverages / Bartending. | COOKING /
    Regional & Ethnic / Scandinavian. | LCGFT: Cookbooks.
Classification: LCC TX722.A1 V65 2018 | DDC 641.5948--dc23
LC record available at https://lccn.loc.gov/2017057360

10 9 8 7 6 5 4 3 2 1

ISBN: 978-0-7603-5793-4

Acquiring Editor: Thom O'Hearn
Project Manager: Jordan Wiklund
Art Director: Laura Drew
Photography: Peter Frank Edwards
Cover and Page Designer: Laura Klynstra

Printed in China

NORTHERN HOSPITALITY

WITH

THE PORTLAND HUNT + ALPINE CLUB

A CELEBRATION OF COCKTAILS, COOKING, AND COMING TOGETHER

ANDREW AND BRIANA VOLK

CONTENTS

FOREWORD

by JEFFREY MORGENTHALER

In 2009 I was given an extraordinary career opportunity: to pack up my life, move to Portland, and take over the bar program at Clyde Common. While I was somewhat familiar with the city—I had lived just two hours south in the college town of Eugene for the past sixteen years—I didn't know many people in Portland. Yet here I was, tasked with hiring for a big, busy bar. Andrew Volk was the first person I hired.

Andrew was a bartender across town and a regular guest at the bar. I loved his professionalism and his dry sense of humor, but I was mainly struck by his Northeastern demeaner. He was calm, cool, and collected. In fact, Andrew was unflappable. When we were back there getting it handed to us on a Friday night, Andrew was cool as a cucumber while I was flailing around like a moth under a hundred-watt bulb.

Briana also became a regular guest at the bar, although she was much more of a fixture after she noticed Andrew had started working there. Briana is the yang to Andrew's yin: outspoken, brassy, and occasionally a little too loud. We all adored her. Briana is a passionate person, full of fire, and eager to share her love of life with everyone around.

Andrew and Briana were almost instantly joined at the hip. Since they were two of my favorite people in town, I soon started spending a lot of my free time with them as well. We would get big groups together for brunch on the weekends, cook dinner with a few friends, or pick up a bunch of hot wings for the Super Bowl. What struck me about Andrew and Briana was their unique take on hospitality and just how effortlessly they assembled a good time with friends.

A lot of people will try to tell you that hospitality and entertaining are predicated on service. They'll tell you that to be a good host, you need to constantly be anticipating your guests' needs—and be prepared to fulfill those needs at any time during the entertainment experience. (It's as if you're a trained culinary professional pretending to relax at home.) Andrew and Briana's hospitality proves that theorem wrong, and it's one of the things that has endeared them to me for most of the past decade. When you're with the Volks, you realize that the very essence of hospitality comes from sharing what you hold closest to your heart with other people. It's obvious when you're in their restaurants, and it's obvious when you're in their home.

What you'll find inside this book is much more than a collection of recipes, although these recipes are as flawless as you'll find anywhere. You'll discover a collection of the things that Andrew and Briana are most passionate about. They've been sharing these drinks, dishes, and stories with their local community for years. Now they're sharing them with the wider world. I'm sure you'll enjoy their hospitality as much as I have.

INTRODUCTION

I met Andrew when he was behind the bar at Clyde Common in Portland, Oregon. He was the cute bartender I flirted with all night as he made me Old Fashioneds. Our first date, a few days later, took us from bar to restaurant to bar to bar before he sang me "We Didn't Start the Fire" on the car ride home at 2 a.m. Since that night, food and drink has been a constant in our lives. We've traveled for hours to eat at former cattle drive stops and wandered cities to find hole-in-the-wall bars that friends of friends recommended. We also cooked like mad. As we combined our friend groups, we would host large dinners that went late into the night. Through the good and the bad, we love to eat and drink.

In late 2011 we moved to Portland, Maine. We didn't move here to open a bar. I was working in advertising as a writer and took the job because Andrew convinced me I'd love it. He was from Vermont and went to college north of Portland, so he knew the area and was excited to get back. Our first apartment was an open, airy loft that overlooked Casco Bay and, beyond that, the Atlantic Ocean. We could walk out our door and be steps away from restaurants that helped put Portland on the culinary map, such as Hugo's and Fore Street. We were also stumbling distance to a neighborhood bar called Sangillo's. It was there, about a year after our arrival, during a blizzard and probably a few too many whiskeys, that the idea of opening a bar came up.

Andrew had been bartending for close to a decade when we started planning opening the Portland Hunt + Alpine Club. The philosophy behind the bar was simple: friendly people making great drinks. We believe that eating and drinking shouldn't be fussy or exclusive; it should be fun. With Hunt + Alpine, we wanted to bring our favorite things about Maine into the space: a love of the outdoors, the cold, good drinks, and the community that is fostered around those things. Embracing my Finnish heritage made sense too; Scandinavian food goes *really* well with drinking, and we can source almost everything we need for our recipes locally. All of these pieces helped create the Portland Hunt + Alpine Club.

On September 5, 2013, we opened the doors. I was three months pregnant with our daughter, Oona, and we really didn't know what to expect. We were two scrappy kids who thought we had a pretty good idea and couldn't wait to share it. In the years since, it has been amazing to watch Hunt + Alpine grow, evolve, and become a space beloved by so many. Yet the root of the place remains the same: friendly people making you great drinks and food. This book is an extension of us and of Hunt + Alpine. We hope you'll find that great drinks don't have to be hard to make, cold drinks can warm you up, anyone can build a fire, and smorgasbords are wonderful. And if you ever come to Maine, we hope you come say hello and see Hunt + Alpine for yourself.

—BRIANA VOLK

CHAPTER 1

WELCOME TO THE
PORTLAND HUNT +
ALPINE CLUB

When you walk in the doors of our restaurant, you're walking into our version of a Maine-meets-Finland ski lodge. It's open and airy, with dark woods, a metal bar top, mounted animal heads made from heavy wire, and a Dutch Golden Age–style painting of a slaughtered rabbit. We built this space to create the bar we always wanted: a place where you can sit in front of some of the best bartenders in the country and geek out, while still finding a way to relax. A place where you can find a quiet corner to seal the deal (whatever that deal may be).

Before we opened, we had a clear vision for the layout and drinks, but we still needed to find the right approach to the food. The kitchen space at Hunt + Alpine helped us with that in its own way: it's tiny. Our kitchen is made up of two induction burners, a small convection oven, and a few tools we love: Vitamix blender, Sunkist juicer, and a meat grinder. (We just might have the smallest professional kitchen in the state.) Still, we wanted the food to be as good as the drinks and to go well with drinking.

When we started diving deep into Scandinavian food, we knew we had our perfect match. Briana grew up in Astoria, Oregon, which is the oldest American settlement west of the Rockies and home to many Scandinavians, including her grandparents who lived across the street from her for years. Growing up, her grandmother and great-grandmother (mummu) would make classic Finnish dishes such as *pulla* (see page 170) and *riccipurra* (see page 87). She had already introduced these dishes to Andrew years ago, but little did we know they'd become the foundation for our menu at Hunt + Alpine. It is hearty food that uses the seasons' bounty, and we just couldn't think of a better cuisine to make, serve, and eat in Maine.

IT'S ALL ABOUT THE EXPERIENCE

For us, building the Hunt + Alpine Club was really about creating a space where we could do what we love the most: creating experiences for people. We serve great drinks and food, but our number one goal is to give people a great experience. You can have the best meal or drink of your life, but if the space is terrible or the service is off, it can change the entire evening. That said, we don't want to be too showy or rely on too many tricks—we strongly believe in finding a balance between wearing the cocktail geek on our sleeve and allowing our guests to enjoy themselves in the space as they see fit. For us, the time, space, and people matter just as much as the food or drink.

One source of inspiration for us is a restaurant in central Oregon called Cowboy Dinner Tree. It was originally a stop off for cattle drives where people could get a warm meal and sleep for the night before moving cattle again in the morning. Now, it's an out-of-the-way restaurant in the Oregon Outback that serves your choice of two main courses—steak or a whole chicken—along with salad, rolls, and a side of beans. But the menu at Cowboy Dinner Tree is beside the point of the place; it's special because of its atmosphere and location. Before we had children, we drove almost five hours one-way to have dinner there, and it was worth every minute. We still talk about taking a trip back with our kids to experience Cowboy Dinner Tree again.

WE LOVE SEXY LIGHTING

During the opening night at Hunt + Alpine, in one of the few moments we stood back and assessed the scene, the restaurant was full of people—and everyone looked great! We think people appreciate attention to lighting, even if they don't think about it. Lighting plays an incredible role in setting the mood, no matter where you are. When you are setting up a room to host a group of people, think about how people and the surrounding spaces will be lit. It can be the detail to simply make your friends look gorgeous after 1 a.m. and more than a few cocktails.

Hunt + Alpine is a big, open space with light-gray walls and high ceilings. It would be easy to over-light the people in the room. To avoid this, lights don't directly shine on any-one. We have lighting at waist height that aims down to the floor and bar pendants that aim up. That means the area where people are sitting is in a diffused zone of soft lighting, and *everyone* looks good in soft lighting. Even our bathroom is cast with a dim light, which helps keep the lighting consistent throughout our space.

LEAVE THEM WANTING MORE
(AND WITH SOMETHING TO TAKE HOME)

Years ago, we used to throw small invite-only events called "Hush, Hush." They were set in places like our loft overlooking Casco Bay, a friend's office after work, or in soon-to-open restaurants. The idea behind them was twofold: to introduce what we do to a wider group of people and to throw a killer party with our chef and spirit industry friends.

At each of these parties, we would always make sure everyone left with something to take along with them. At one, which featured spirits made by a former beekeeper, we sent guests home with jars of honey from the beekeeper's hives. At another we set up a large prize wheel, and guests took turns spinning it. Prizes ranged from shirts and sunglasses to things that were more experiential, such as laybacks (where someone lies down on a table or bench and has a shot poured into their mouth). Beyond just being fun, "Hush, Hush," and these small moments within each party, showed our guests enough to know there was plenty more to be had and much more beneath the surface of what we were planning with Hunt + Alpine.

When you provide a little something that guests can take with them, they are left with a physical reminder of the great time they had. And, if you're stuck thinking of something, doughnuts are a never-fail way to excite guests as they walk out the door. It puts this killer endcap on an already great night. The best bonfires, dinners, and parties are always made better by something a little unexpected.

FIRECRACKER

This drink was on our opening menu and has reappeared frequently over the years. It's one of those drinks that are popular with a wide range of people, as it's easy to drink. It's also incredibly easy to make! While we don't mind substitutions in some cocktails, for this one you really do need to track down Royal Rose's Three Chile Simple Syrup. Made in small batches here in Maine by a husband-and-wife team, it has the perfect amount of heat and complexity. Once you have it on hand, you're sure to find other uses for it as well. Do yourself a favor and pick it up if you're making this cocktail.

YIELD: 1 DRINK ⚜ **GLASS: COLLINS**

1½ ounces vodka

¾ ounce Royal Rose Three Chile Simple Syrup

¾ ounce fresh lime juice

Soda water, to fill (approximately 3 ounces)

Lime wheel, for garnish

Combine the vodka, syrup, and lime juice in a mixing tin.

Add ice, cap the tin, and shake vigorously for 30 seconds.

Strain into a Collins glass. Fill the glass with fresh ice and top with soda water. Garnish with the lime wheel.

WHEN TO SHAKE, STIR, OR BLEND YOUR COCKTAIL

One of the most common questions we get asked at Hunt + Alpine is why we shake one cocktail and stir another. When you shake, stir, or blend a drink, you are changing it in three important ways: temperature, dilution, and texture. Adding ice in any method will obviously chill your drink, and there are plenty of technical discussions out there about how efficient each preparation is in chilling your drink. For our purposes, know that it's best to keep your ice as cold as possible. Just as obvious, adding frozen water to your cocktail is going to dilute it. Dilution is a good thing, as it softens the harsh edges on straight spirits, yet too much water in a drink can ruin it as well.

The biggest factor in deciding what to do comes down to texture. When you stir a drink, the resulting cocktail is silky, rich, and incredibly pleasant. When you shake a drink, the motion of shaking with ice cubes adds tiny air bubbles that create a zippy, light, and frothy texture. When you blend, the ice cubes are pulverized to a slushy consistency. This should be considered when thinking about the goal of your cocktail. The rules we use are as follows, but as with any rule, once you learn to apply them correctly, feel free to choose to contradict them. We certainly do. For example, the Fratelli Stinger (page 105) is a drink that by all rights should be stirred, but we shake them.

Let's start with the one rule everyone learns on this topic: drinks with clear ingredients are stirred (think martinis and Manhattans). This is 100 percent a textural choice; some people prefer their martinis shaken. For us, a silky, rich, smooth martini is so much better than one with ice shards and air bubbles on top.

Next up, drinks with citrus, eggs, or cream should be shaken. Because shaking with ice (the harder and larger the cubes, the better) adds tiny air bubbles, those bubbles lend the entire drink a frothy texture that cuts the textural weight of citrus, eggs, or cream on the palate. When shaking a drink, you'll usually want to strain the drink with a fine-mesh strainer (also called fine straining). This removes the small shards of ice that have been shaken from the cubes. These shards add a textural element that is unwelcome in most drinks. Again, there are reasons to break this rule, but normally we fine strain all shaken drinks.

Blend drinks only by design, as blended drinks tend to require double (at least) the sugar component of any drink in its unblended form. See our daiquiri recipes on page 183 for an example.

One of the yardsticks that bartenders use to discuss these rules and drink composition in general is a fresh juice daiquiri. Daiquiris, while popularized in the United States through blended, sweet, and fruity variations, at their core have three ingredients—rum, lime juice, and sugar. With such a simple composition, there is little room to hide flavors or poor preparation, yet there's still plenty of room to make the drink your own. Which rum (or blend of rums) do you use? How much sugar and juice do you use? Do you like the drink sweet or tart? What type of sugar is used? Is the drink shaken or blended? If shaken, what kind of ice is used? Many rules are meant to be broken, however. Use them as a starting point for your own explorations.

A PRICE ABOVE RUBIES

Low-alcohol, bubbly cocktails are the perfect drinks to offer guests as they come into your home. A Price above Rubies is one of those crowd pleasers that bourbon lovers will enjoy, but it is light enough for fans of all things bubbly. The splash of amaro creates an amazing balance between the bourbon and bubbles as well. These are especially wonderful predinner drinks because they stimulate the appetite, and you don't have to worry about anyone getting tipsy before food is served.

YIELD: 1 DRINK ⋄ **GLASS: CHAMPAGNE FLUTE**

---

1 ounce bourbon

¾ ounce fresh lemon juice

½ ounce amaro Montenegro

½ ounce rich simple syrup (see page 191)

4 ounces sparkling white wine

Lemon peel, for garnish

Combine the bourbon, lemon juice, amaro Montenegro, and syrup in a mixing tin.

Add ice, cap the tin, and shake vigorously for 30 seconds.

Fine strain into a champagne flute. Top with the sparkling wine. Express the lemon peel over the drink, and then use it as a garnish.

LUNAR PHASES

This drink was the Pacific Northwest regional winner for Tanqueray's "Best Gin & Tonic" contest many, many years ago. You'll find the Lunar Phases is a welcoming and pleasant riff on what's usually just a two-ingredient drink. Sure, it takes a bit more work than tossing gin and tonic into a glass, but we think it is well worth it.

YIELD: 1 DRINK ⚬ GLASS: CHILLED COCKTAIL

1½ ounces London dry gin (preferably Tanqueray)

½ ounce fresh lime juice

½ ounce Cocchi Americano (you can substitute Lillet blanc)

½ ounce quinine syrup (recipe follows)

2 ounces sparkling white wine

Combine the gin, lime juice, Cocchi Americano, and syrup in a mixing tin.

Fill the tin with ice, cap, and shake hard for 30 to 45 seconds.

Fine strain into a chilled cocktail glass. Top with the sparkling wine.

QUININE SYRUP

This syrup is simple to make. It also opens up possibilities for cocktails, since you can add the quinine flavor without adding the sparkling water component of bottled tonic water. Feel free to play with the botanicals depending on your preference, except for the cinchona bark, which is one of the few places quinine is found in nature. You must use the bark and can find it dried at many herbal stores online. We prefer to use the large chunks as opposed to the powder, as we feel it gives us more control over the bitterness.

YIELD: 750ML OR 3½ CUPS

½ cup cinchona bark, roughly cut

1 whole orange, peel only

1 whole grapefruit, peel only

⅓ cup agave syrup

⅓ cup sugar

¼ teaspoon citric acid

Heat 3 cups water in a medium saucepan until almost boiling. Remove the pan from the heat, and add the cinchona bark, orange peel, and grapefruit peel. Steep for 20 minutes, covered. Fine strain into a mixing bowl. Mix in the agave, sugar, and citric acid. Once the sugar is fully dissolved, bottle, label, and refrigerate. This syrup keeps for well over a month in the fridge.

To make tonic water, pour ¾ ounce syrup in a double old fashioned glass. Fill the glass with ice, top with soda water and a squeeze of lime, and stir.

GREEN CHILE POPCORN

We're a Scandinavian-influenced cocktail bar that's known for its spicy popcorn. If that doesn't make sense to you, it will after you try this recipe—it's really good popcorn! We have tried other versions over the years, but nothing has been quite as good, or as popular, as this one. It's so popular that the movie theater a block away has asked us to stop serving it to go because moviegoers were ordering it and then sneaking it into the theater. Now, we're not saying that's what you should do, but when you serve this, make sure you have plenty, because it will go fast.

YIELD: APPROXIMATELY 8 CUPS

---

6 tablespoons butter, divided

¼ cup white corn kernels

1 teaspoon salt, or to taste

1 tablespoon powdered green chile (available in some grocery stores and online), or to taste

⅓ cup powdered Parmesan cheese, divided

Heat a large heavy-bottomed pot (one with a lid) over medium-low heat, adding 3 tablespoons butter as the pot warms. The pot should be big enough to hold two times your final yield; for the above recipe as written, the pot should hold at least 16 cups to allow enough room for the popcorn to expand.

In a second, smaller pot, melt the other 3 tablespoons butter and set aside.

Once the butter in the large pot has melted and any bubbling has subsided, add the corn kernels to the pot, give it a shake to coat the kernels in butter, and cover the pot with the lid. Increase the heat to medium. As the kernels start to pop, gently agitate the pot to keep the kernels moving. The idea here is to make sure all the kernels are evenly distributed and heated.

As the popping increases, continue to gently agitate the pot, allowing the popped corn to rise to the top and unpopped kernels to fall to the bottom and continue to pop. If you've ever made popcorn in the microwave, you'll recognize this next step: Pay attention to the regularity of the popping. Once you can count to five (slowly) between pops, the popcorn is done.

Quickly remove the pot from the heat and dump the popcorn into a bowl that's large enough to toss the popcorn around. Alternatively, you can use a heavy-duty brown paper bag and fold over the top to shake the contents. Gently pour the reserved melted butter from the small pot over the popcorn. Sprinkle the salt, the powdered green chile, and half the cheese over the popped corn, and toss to coat. Taste and adjust the seasoning as desired.

Serve in a large bowl and sprinkle the remaining cheese over the top of the popcorn just before serving.

MIXED NUTS

Wonderfully shareable, these nuts have a couple of unexpected elements: Aleppo chili and Angostura bitters (which has plenty of other uses in this book). One of our favorite things about this recipe is that it works year round. The flavors are bright, and the heat gives it warmth. When you don't have a lot of time to make a starter or snack, this is something that you can whip up in a pinch. Additionally, the nuts can be made in advance and kept on hand, ready at a moment's notice for an impromptu snack.

YIELD: 3 CUPS

1 cup raw, unsalted almonds	**1½ teaspoons Angostura bitters**
1 cup raw, unsalted pistachios	**1 teaspoon Aleppo chili powder**
1 cup shelled walnut halves	**½ teaspoon powdered cinnamon**
2 teaspoons honey	**1 teaspoon sea salt, or to taste**

Preheat the oven to 450°F.

Spread the nuts evenly on a large rimmed baking sheet. Place the tray on the middle rack. Roast the nuts until fragrant and a pleasant light brown color, about 10 minutes. While roasting, shake the tray about every 5 minutes to agitate the nuts. Rotate the baking sheet if needed to ensure even heat distribution.

Once the nuts are done, immediately transfer them to a bowl and add the honey, bitters, chili powder, cinnamon, and salt. Toss as you add these ingredients to make sure you evenly coat the nuts in honey and spices. Taste and adjust the seasoning to your liking.

Serve immediately. This recipe will keep for up to 2 weeks in an airtight container.

MIXED OLIVES

The biggest fan of this snack just might be our three-year-old daughter, Oona. We've watched her sneak these from the table at parties and at the restaurant! They are a perfect make-ahead snack that you can warm as needed. In fact, the longer they sit, the better they get.

YIELD: 4 CUPS

4 cups mixed olives (pitted or unpitted), packed in oil

2 oranges

½ teaspoon red pepper flakes

3 sprigs fresh thyme

Place the olives, along with the oil they were packed in, in a large, sealable mixing container. Finely zest both oranges, and add the zest to the container with the olives. Quarter 1 orange and, by hand, squeeze the juice from each quarter into the mixing container. Toss the spent quarters into the container as well.

Add the red pepper flakes and thyme springs to the olives, then mix well to incorporate. Seal the container and allow everything to rest, refrigerated, for at least 48 hours. This will keep, refrigerated, for up to 1 month.

Before heating and serving, remove the thyme springs and orange pieces. Transfer the olives to a heatproof container, such as a glass baking dish, and heat in a 200°F oven for 20 minutes to warm through.

Serve immediately, with small dishes on the side if the olives have not been pitted.

1840 SAZERAC

The Sazerac is one of the oldest cocktails in existence, dating back to the 1800s in the French Quarter of New Orleans. Its recipe and story have been faithfully passed down through generations of bartenders. It has stood the test of time, even surviving Prohibition intact. What often is left out of the barroom version of the Sazerac story is that it was initially made with cognac instead of rye whiskey as its base. In the 1850s and 1860s, the most desirable spirit to drink among the wealthy was cognac, as nearly everything French was in vogue at the time. Cognac was readily available and imported by numerous agents, including a brand called Sazerac de Forge et Fils. It is thought that from this brand (along with a coffeehouse of the same name, which served the cocktail) comes the name for the drink. Not long after, in 1863, a tiny pest called phylloxera started decimating the grapevines in France; it is estimated that between 1863 and 1875, two-thirds of all grapevines were destroyed by the bug. With the destruction of France's grapes came the skyrocketing of prices of any grape-based product, including cognac. When cognac became increasingly more difficult to obtain, the readily available rye whiskey was used to create the Sazerac, which is the recipe that is most used today (with a small amount of Angostura bitters to round out the drink). In this cocktail, we stick to the classic specs handed down by Thomas Handy but go back and swap the phenomenal Pierre Ferrand 1840 cognac in for rye whiskey.

YIELD: 1 DRINK ⚜ GLASS: CHILLED SINGLE OLD FASHIONED

---

2 ounces Pierre Ferrand 1840 cognac

2 dashes Angostura bitters

5 dashes Peychaud's bitters

1 teaspoon rich simple syrup (see page 191)

Absinthe, for glass rinse

Lemon peel

Combine the cognac, Angostura bitters, Peychaud's bitters, and syrup in a mixing glass.

Rinse a chilled single old fashioned glass with a small amount of absinthe, or use 3 pumps from a small atomizer to mist the chilled glass with the aroma of absinthe. Set the chilled, absinthe-rinsed glass aside.

Add ice to the mixing glass and stir 30 to 50 times.

Gently strain the drink into the chilled single old fashioned glass. Express the lemon peel across the top of the drink and discard.

THE ABSINTHE ATOMIZER

If you don't like the flavor of absinthe, you can still add a hint of the aroma you need for some cocktail recipes. You'll just need a small plastic atomizer bottle with a pump top. Fill the bottle with absinthe and spritz three times instead of giving the glass a rinse. This can also come in handy as a garnish or light finishing touch for many drinks, including our Late Night at OOB (see page 177).

PUTTING TOGETHER A COCKTAIL MENU

One of the more difficult skills in bartending is often an afterthought in training programs. There is much attention paid (and rightfully so) to the physical techniques of how to build a drink, the varying differences among amari, and how to properly balance a cocktail's ingredients. Yet how to effectively create a cocktail menu is often overlooked by bar managers and bartenders across the country. There is so much to talk about here that you could put together an entire class on this and not nearly cover it all; in fact, Andrew presented a two-hour class on this exact topic at the Bar Institute with our friend Will Thompson, and we ended up cutting out half the content because we couldn't do it all justice. Luckily, it's a bit simpler when it comes to writing a cocktail menu for an event at home. Here are some broad guidelines to stick to when it comes to making a beautiful, efficient, and effective menu for your next party.

Start with an honest assessment of your abilities as well as the facilities where you'll be making drinks. Think about how much time you want to spend making drinks versus interacting with your guests. If you are the sole host, there are going to be numerous other duties, so keep the options limited and easy to produce—either by you or with instructions for your guests. Our favorite option here is to put out a large pitcher of something prebatched, such as the White Noise (see page 51), an ice bucket, and a handful of glasses, along with a sign that simply says "Pour Me"). If you're going to have time to bartend but are working off of a small side table, maybe save the twelve-ingredient cocktail for another night so you don't overclutter your workstation. Additionally, assess how familiar you are with creating drinks in a new space. Even the best bartenders in the world make clumsy mistakes working behind a new bar.

Another very important factor in writing a cocktail menu is your guests' varying preferences. It can come as a surprise to many newly indoctrinated bartenders that not everyone shares their love of Italian digestifs or barrel-proof bourbons. There are many more guests out there now who want those things than a decade ago, but there are still guests who want something lighter, fruitier, or less palate pounding. The menu that you are writing for your party should be representative of you and what you want to offer, but at the same time, you are creating offerings for everyone you've invited. If you don't know whether or not all of your friends are going to enjoy your Manhattan variation with housemade bitters and overproof rum, include a lighter option or two for their sake. It never hurts to have some cans of lighter beer or a bottle of rosé on hand as well; our fridge is rarely without both a six-pack of local, sessionable beer and a chilled bottle of rosé at the ready.

When writing a cocktail menu for an event or a party, take into consideration what else is being served. Have you made everything for a true Scandinavian-style smorgasbord? Then serve drinks that are going to go well with cured meats, fish, sandwiches, and pickles. A clean, high-proof option would work well (such as a Gibson, see page 107), as would some quaffable quenchers such as the White Noise (see page 51). Or are you serving guests smoked meats? Something bolder would be right at home, such as the Anthology Club (see page 73) or a Firecracker (see page 4).

Finally, one of our favorite parts about writing a menu is not just placing a bunch of great drinks together, but also thinking about how those drinks can tell a story with each other. Think about the thread that weaves through all of your options, and use that as a unifying theme. It can certainly be simple—drinks containing one spirit, for example—but don't shy away from something more obscure if it strikes you. One of our favorites was a Tom Waits–inspired menu that our friends Phoebe Esmon and Christian Gaal put together. On its own, every drink tasted great, but the fact that each was inspired by various Waits lyrics tied everything together beautifully.

ÆBLESKIVER

Shareable desserts can be difficult to make and serve. They need to be either quite large or a bunch of small treats to be served individually. These little "donuts" are a great alternative; you can make any size batch you want, and the serving couldn't be easier. Just stack them on a large platter on top of a linen towel to help keep some heat on the bottom without making them soggy. Our favorite way to eat these is while they are still warm, with a berry jam that brings out their pancake-like qualities. Dusting them with powdered sugar or using warm Maine maple syrup for dipping are good decisions as well.

YIELD: APPROXIMATELY 2 DOZEN SMALL ÆBLESKIVER

11 tablespoons unsalted butter, divided, plus more to coat pan

1 cup whole milk

2 tablespoons sugar

1 orange, zested

1 package (0.25 ounce) instant yeast

2 cups all-purpose flour

3 eggs

Salt

In a saucepan over medium-low heat, melt 7 tablespoons butter. Once the butter melts, add the milk. Once the milk begins to warm, but before it begins to bubble, add the sugar, orange zest, yeast, and a pinch of salt, stirring until everything dissolves. Do not allow the milk to simmer or boil as you do this.

Remove the pot from the heat and mix in the flour. Once the flour is incorporated, add the eggs and stir just until everything is well blended.

Grease a mixing bowl with butter and place the dough in it, covering it with a clean dish towel. Let the dough rise for 30 minutes.

In a cast-iron skillet or your preferred pan, heat the remaining 4 tablespoons butter over medium-high heat until it melts and bubbles at the edges. Before the butter begins to brown, using 2 spoons, shape the dough into small balls and carefully drop them into the pan. Make as many at a time as fit into the pan, leaving about 1 inch of space between them. Turn them as needed so they cook evenly on all sides. Add more butter as necessary between batches.

Serve warm with jam or condiments of your choice.

SIMA

Every June, in Briana's hometown of Astoria, Oregon, there is a Scandinavian midsummer festival. As a child, she would go with her grandparents to watch the traditional dancers, see who would be crowned Miss Scandinavia (always rooting for the Finnish entrant), and go booth to booth to sample the locally made treats. One of her favorite booths served a traditional Finnish fermented lemonade called *sima*. We think you'll also love the slightly yeasty flavor, sweetness, and effervescence, as well as the raisins that will bob around your cup. When fermenting this drink, if you go longer than recommended in the instructions, it will start to become mildly alcoholic, so keep the fermentation to the bare minimum if you don't want it to become boozy. You can use the non-alcoholic sima as a cocktail mixer, as it goes well with both vodka and bourbon.

YIELD: 8 TO 12 SERVINGS (APPROXIMATELY 1 GALLON)

---

2 large lemons

½ cup dark brown sugar

½ cup granulated sugar

1 package (0.25 ounce) instant yeast

1 cup golden raisins

Zest the lemons, then slice them into thin wheels. Remove any seeds.

Combine, in a heat-proof bowl, the lemon wheels, zest, and both sugars to create an oleo-saccharum. Let rest for 1 hour.

In a large pot, bring 1 gallon water to a boil. Carefully add the boiling water to the oleo-saccharum and mix until all sugars are dissolved. Let cool until just warm to the touch (approximately 100ºF), then stir in the yeast.

Cover the mixture with plastic wrap and let sit at room temperature for 24 hours. The top of the liquid should be foamy.

Using a fine-mesh strainer, strain the liquid into multiple jars or bottles. You can use any airtight containers, from mason jars to wine bottles with corks—even Pyrex will work just fine. Divide the golden raisins equally among the containers, then seal the containers.

Refrigerate the containers and check them daily. When most or all of the raisins have floated to the top, it's done. This usually takes 2 to 3 days.

Unseal the containers right before serving, as the sima will lose its effervescence if you open the containers too early. If you leave the containers sealed longer than 3 days, the yeast will continue to work, and the sima will become slightly alcoholic.

CHAPTER 2

THE SEA AND SALTY AIR

Maine has more coastline than any other state. If you stretched it out, with all its islands and inlets, you'd be able to lay it across the entire United States. We love going out and discovering what the coast has to offer. From family-friendly beaches to artist colonies on islands that don't allow cars, it seems like we could spend our whole life exploring this state.

One of our favorite memories is two nights we spent on Monhegan Island. It's an artist community a few miles off the coast by ferry, no outside cars are allowed, and it has only one inn. At any given time, there are no more than five hundred inhabitants. Monhegan has been the inspiration for artists such as Andrew Wyeth and Rockwell Kent. We spent our time on the island walking from edge to edge; the western side, where the inn is located, is the center of the community. With small shops, galleries, and a couple of restaurants, this is where the ferry drops you off. The eastern side is very different; you can hike through a forest to the edge of a cliff where the Atlantic lies as far as you can see. Spending even a day there, you will understand why this place has inspired so many people.

For us, the Maine coast has inspired many cocktails. Living so close to the ocean means that when we step out of our house, we can smell the sea and salt in the air. The ocean is an essential part of our lives. We love to gather seawater to make martinis, using salt as an ingredient beyond the rim of a glass. One of the drinks that will most likely go down as a Hunt + Alpine all-time classic, Green Eyes, makes us think of salt water, foggy nights, and little port towns.

Of course, the ocean and coast have an enormous impact on our food as well. The working waterfront is just steps from Hunt + Alpine, which means we purchase fresh fish, oysters, and lobster from our neighbors. Unlike so many coastal towns that have a large tourist draw, our docks still serve the fishermen, as they have for generations. That means our waterfront is one of the first places we send visitors so they can see the men and women who go out every day to bring in the food we eat. In a similar spirit, we suggest hopping a ride on the Casco Bay Lines Mailboat. Bring a bottle of wine and a picnic as you ride this working mail ferry, going from island to island dropping off the mail. There is something so magical about riding a real, working boat for three hours and seeing just a little snippet of island life. It is one of our favorite things to do when we have a free afternoon.

ALL ABOUT OYSTERS

One of the great things about living as far north as we do is our access to oysters. Maine waters make some of the best oysters in the world—hands down. The frigid, briny sea creates a surprisingly wide variety too, so when we go to our local fishmonger, we love grabbing a variety of options.

It may seem like a luxury to serve oysters in your home, but there isn't a better way to get people involved than setting up an oyster bar inside your kitchen or in your backyard. Shucking oysters isn't as hard as it seems either. Once you try a couple on your own, you'll be able to shuck anytime—and even teach those new to shucking. We do recommend investing in an oyster knife. It is an essential and cheap tool.

HOW TO SHUCK AN OYSTER

STEP 1: First, get a pile of ice ready to keep your oysters cold while shucking. If you're on the beach or lake instead of in the kitchen, your oysters should be kept inside a cooler. Oysters are living creatures that can drown, which is why they must be kept on ice, not in water, with air able to flow around them. If you're traveling with oysters, make sure they are raised off the floor of the cooler sufficiently to prevent them from drowning as the ice melts.

STEP 2: Using a kitchen towel folded into thirds lengthwise, grip the oyster firmly with your nondominant hand. You'll need to keep it steady when you're shucking. The towel can also help protect your hand in case your knife slips. Oysters have a top and bottom; the belly side is the bottom and the flat side is the top. Place your oyster in the towel, belly side down, nestled in the towel. You only want the hinge of the oyster exposed.

STEP 3: Use an oyster knife to gently pry apart the hinge of the oyster. Going in too hard can cause the shell to break or cause your knife to slip. Start twisting into the hinge gently until you find that you can pry it apart. As you continue to twist the knife, the shell should come apart.

STEP 4: Slide your knife along the bottom part of the top shell to release the muscle that's holding the shells together. Once you do that, you'll be able to take the top shell off. Keep the oyster level to the ground to avoid spilling any liquid from the shell.

STEP 5: Throw out the top shell and make sure there aren't any shell fragments in the bottom shell. You do not want to eat those!

STEP 6: Finally, gently slide your knife under the oyster so it detaches from the bottom shell. Be careful not to cut into the oyster. It's now ready to eat!

We like to eat oysters straight out of the shell as we shuck them, with nothing more than a squirt of lemon. However, grilling them in the half shell is a great way to get anyone who might be squeamish of raw seafood to eat them—and it's also pretty delicious.

Think your kids won't eat oysters? Think again. Oysters are weird looking, their shells are bumpy, they smell like the ocean, and they are kind of slimy. It's perfect kid stuff. If you start kids out eating them when they are little, it's going to become second nature. When she was just a year old, we took our daughter, Oona, to Eventide here in Portland to try her first oyster. We chose the small, briny Wild Damariscotta and let her figure out what to do all on her own. She loved it, and now at three easily eats half a dozen on her own! When our son, Rocky, turns one, you'll find us back at Eventide.

OYSTER PAIRINGS

You can't go wrong pairing oysters with white wine, bubbles, or sherry. Yet, while we are often purists when it comes to topping our oysters, we can definitely get behind pairing oysters with a wide variety of things to drink—and even some shooters. At Hunt + Alpine, we've done extensive hands-on research. Here are our findings.

WINE: It's not exactly groundbreaking to say that there are some phenomenal wines practically designed to be paired with oysters, but it's often either an overlooked opportunity or simply not a thoughtful choice. Some classics when it comes to wine are muscadet, or anything bubbly and dry, be it a cava, prosecco, crémant, or champagne. If it's a bit cool out, don't be shy about pulling out a bottle of red instead. Personally we keep it on the lighter side (a French-style gamay or pinot noir would do well here), and we would certainly put a little chill on the red wine before opening it.

SHERRY: This wine category deserves its own section. If you're not familiar with sherry or you think of it as something that only your grandmother drinks, it's time to correct that immediately. To those in the know, sherry is a special, delicious category of wine that is often easy to find at a reasonable price. There are dozens of books that detail the categories of sherry, but for our purposes, it helps to know that there are multiple styles that range in flavor from salty, clean, and lean to nutty, caramel-like, and quite sweet. When pairing with oysters, you want to reach for something on the leaner side; we always keep a chilled bottle of either fino or manzanilla in our refrigerator.

BEER: Pairing options here can go one of two ways. You can opt for a quaffable, sessionable beer such as a European-style lager or pilsner, or you can grab something dry with dark malts, such as an Irish-style stout. Both options will pair beautifully with a couple dozen oysters. We generally recommend avoiding beers with a prominent hop profile to them (such as IPAs), as the bitterness can overpower the little guys. But when eating oysters, we very much love the toasted malt profile that comes through in a Guinness, or the thirst-quenching power of some of our local lighter options (Bunker's Machine and Oxbow's Luppolo, both pilsners, come to mind).

Continued on next page

SPIRITS, COCKTAILS, AND SHOOTERS: Try oysters with a classic gin martini. Sure, there are other options, but you need to at least start with the classic! Ready to move on? Shooters are where pairing can get its most creative. While we still recommend sticking to flavors that are lighter so as not to overpower the oysters, making your own shooter is a great start to a party and allows you to explore your wild side. The idea here is that you make and chill a liquor or mix that can be poured into shot glasses and then shuck as many oysters as there are shots. Rest an oyster shell, still full, on each shot glass. Everyone shoots the oyster first and chases it with the liquor afterwards. The shooter can be as easy (a bottle of chilled vodka or aquavit pulled from the freezer, for example) or as complicated as you'd like. Here are a few suggestions:

- Vodka and any pickle brine (liquid from pickled red onion would be particularly great here), mixed two parts to one part
- Tequila and your favorite hot sauce, perhaps a dash or two per shot
- Brown Butter–Washed Aquavit (see page 131), pulled straight from the freezer
- Irish whiskey and a small amount of kimchi liquid, approximately six parts to one part

SHRUBS: If you're looking for a nonalcoholic option to share with the kids or simply to make sure your afternoon get-together doesn't turn into an all-night rager, it's helpful to have a shrub or two on hand to use alongside oysters as a shooter. Shrubs, generally, are sweetened vinegar-and-fruit concoctions that are delicious on their own, lengthened with soda water, or mixed into cocktails. Making a shrub is as easy as combining equal amounts of vinegar and sugar (by weight or by volume) and using that mixture to generously cover your fruit base. Allow that to sit in a covered container in your refrigerator overnight (or longer), and then strain the solids away. Initially developed as a preservation method before refrigeration, shrubs will keep indefinitely when chilled. Here's an easy summer recipe to pair with oysters: Mix 1 pound clean, hulled strawberries with 1 cup good-quality cider vinegar and 1 cup sugar. Gently crush the fruit and allow to sit, covered, overnight in your refrigerator. Strain away the solids, making sure to save as much liquid from the fruit as possible. Bottle the liquid and refrigerate. You can use it straight as a shooter for oysters, though a dash of hot sauce wouldn't hurt either.

GREEN EYES

Inspired by the salty ocean that's just steps from our door, the mix of Chartreuse and gin along with the texture of the egg whites in this drink makes it a sister of the sea. To say it's popular would be an understatement; it's easily one of the most ordered and photographed drinks we have. (One wedding reception chose to host at Hunt + Alpine because they loved this drink so much!) It is also one of our favorite ways to introduce Chartreuse to our guests. While the spirit is bitter, in this drink it is well balanced by the other ingredients.

YIELD: 1 DRINK ❧ GLASS: CHILLED DOUBLE OLD FASHIONED

1½ ounces gin (we use London dry)

¾ ounce Green Chartreuse

¾ ounce fresh lime juice

½ ounce rich simple syrup (see page 191)

½ ounce egg white

Lime wheel and cocktail cherry, for garnish

Combine the gin, Chartreuse, lime juice, syrup, and egg white in a mixing tin.

Fill the tin with ice, cap, and shake hard for 30 to 45 seconds.

Uncap the tin and fine strain the contents into the empty top of the tin. When you're finished straining, dump all the spent ice from the bottom, transfer the liquid back to the tin, cap, and shake without ice for 10 seconds. This further emulsifies the ingredients to ensure that the drink doesn't separate when served.

Pour the twice-shaken drink into a chilled double old fashioned glass. Fill with fresh ice, garnish with the lime wheel and cherry, and serve.

NOTE: *At Hunt + Alpine, we collect a dozen egg whites and gently whisk them to break down the protein structure. Then we transfer them to a squeeze bottle. You should plan to do something similar if you're making many of these for a party. Otherwise, just use 1 whole egg white and increase the rich simple syrup slightly, as most eggs have a little more than ½ ounce of white.*

HEAVY WEATHER

Vodka as a spirit raises some complicated feelings among bartenders. Some hate using vodka on principle (it is, by definition, flavorless), yet so many people love to drink it. To make things worse, newly invented vodka-based cocktails are often uninspired, overcomplicated, or both. Our goal is always to put in front of someone a drink that they want to drink, not what we think they should be drinking. And frankly, we very much enjoy vodka, especially on the rocks in a chilled glass after a long day of work. Our bar manager, Trey Hughes, came up with this brilliant little number. It is smooth and refreshing, and unlike many vodka drinks, it's not overly sweet. The mix of fresh fruit juices and allspice is unexpected, but we found this has a broad appeal to almost every palate.

YIELD: 1 DRINK ⚬ GLASS: CHILLED DOUBLE OLD FASHIONED

1½ ounces vodka

¾ ounce fresh grapefruit juice

½ ounce fresh lime juice

½ ounce rich simple syrup (see page 191)

1 teaspoon allspice dram (we use St. Elizabeth's, but you can substitute the Hunt + Alpine Cardamom-Coriander Syrup on page 74)

Cocktail cherry, on an umbrella, for garnish

Combine the vodka, grapefruit juice, lime juice, syrup, and allspice dram in a mixing tin.

Fill the tin with ice, cap, and shake hard for 30 to 45 seconds.

Fine strain the drink into a chilled double old fashioned glass. Fill the glass with fresh ice, garnish with the umbrella, and serve.

HUNT + ALPINE'S
PIMM'S CUP

Pimm's is a distinctly English product, a mixture of flavorings and gin (though the now-discontinued Nos. 2 through 6 used other bases, such as Scotch whiskey, brandy, rum, rye, and vodka). The Pimm's Cup cocktail and its multiple variations (using lemonade, ginger ale, tonic, and so on) have English origins as well. However, much of the United States' cocktail history can be traced through the city of New Orleans at some point or another. In the 1950s, a Pimm's Cup recipe found its way into the hands of the proprietor of the Napoleon House in New Orleans, and it quickly became the signature drink of that venerable bar as well—and a staple of bar crawling as you walk through the French Quarter.

We worked on this particular recipe with a New Orleans bartender who spent a couple of months working with us in Maine. Pimm's Cups the world over are intended to be low in alcohol and refreshing on a hot day, and they are supposed to show off the bounty of fresh fruit and other ingredients in their garnishes. The raspberry and ginger syrups bring a depth and zest to the drink that really heighten the experience without changing it. Additionally, the saline solution brings the sweetness back in check. And at Hunt + Alpine, we've been known to go a bit nuts on the garnish when we get our farmers' deliveries of summer fruit.

YIELD: 1 DRINK ⸰ GLASS: COLLINS

1 ounce Pimm's No. 1 Cup

1 ounce gin (we use Beefeater)

¾ ounce fresh lemon juice

½ ounce rich simple syrup (see page 191)

½ ounce raspberry syrup (we prefer the one from our friends at Royal Rose)

¼ ounce ginger syrup (see page 79)

6 drops saline solution (4 parts water to 1 part salt, see Glossary on page 190)

2 to 3 cucumber rounds

Soda water, to fill

Mint, cucumber, and whatever other fresh produce you're excited about, for garnish

Combine the Pimm's, gin, lemon juice, rich simple syrup, raspberry syrup, ginger syrup, saline solution, and cucumber rounds in a mixing tin.

Fill the tin with ice, cap, and shake hard for 30 to 45 seconds.

Fine strain into a Collins glass, then fill the glass with ice and top with soda water. Garnish and serve. For the garnish, be as creative as you like. We often poke the mint through the center of the cucumber round and present it like a boutonniere on the glass.

SALMON SOUP

Our chef created this luxurious and ridiculously easy recipe for a coursed dinner we presented at the James Beard House and refined at our kitchen at Hunt + Alpine. With our tiny kitchen, we often make this soup in very small batches to order. Here, we have built this recipe so you can make it for a crowd rather than one at a time. That said, feel free to scale it up or down—it's quite flexible.

YIELD: 4 ENTRÉE-SIZED SERVINGS

1 cup (approximately ½ pound) fingerling potatoes, chopped into 1-inch rounds

1 tablespoon canola oil, or other unflavored cooking oil

2 leeks, white parts only, roughly chopped

1 large onion, finely diced

¼ teaspoon ground allspice

Pinch of white pepper

1 cup dry white wine

4 teaspoons fish sauce

1½ quarts heavy cream

½ pound raw salmon, skin removed, chopped into 1-inch pieces

Dried seaweed, for garnish

Dill, for garnish

Salt

Bring a small pot of water with a pinch of salt to a boil. Once the water is at a rolling boil, add the potatoes and cook for 10 minutes, or until just fork tender. Be careful not to overcook, as you want them to hold their shape. Turn off the burner, drain the potatoes, and set them aside.

Heat the oil in a medium-size heavy-bottomed saucepan over medium heat. Once the oil is nice and hot, add the leeks and onions and sauté until translucent, about 5 minutes. Add the allspice and white pepper, stirring until they coat the onions and leeks.

Add the white wine, bring the mixture to a boil, and cook until reduced by half, about 3 minutes. Add the fish sauce and heavy cream and immediately reduce the heat to medium low. At this point you don't want to bring the soup to a boil again—keep it at a low simmer.

Add the salmon and cook until just done, approximately 5 minutes. Add the potatoes and warm through.

Divide equally into four bowls, ensuring that each gets a good amount of salmon and potatoes. Garnish with dried seaweed and dill.

REMEMBER THE MAINE

One of the many colorful figures in cocktail history is Charles H. Baker Jr., a world traveler and man of many means who authored *The Gentleman's Companion*, published originally in 1939. Many of Baker's recipes themselves are of questionable origin and balance, often requiring re-apportioning of the ingredients to make them pleasing to a modern palate. However, Baker's ability to tell a story and contextualize drinks in his travels is captivating, allowing us to forgive any details that don't quite work.

Baker recounts sipping this drink in Havana Harbor during the 1933 Cuban Revolution. The drink itself is named for the rallying cry that launched the United States into the Spanish-American War almost forty years earlier, in 1898. Early that year, the battleship USS *Maine* was sent to Havana to protect the United States' interests during another Cuban uprising. The ship exploded under still mysterious circumstances, but the incident was used in the press as a rallying cry: "Remember the *Maine*! To hell with Spain!" Baker surely recalled the wreckage at the bottom of Havana Harbor in 1933 during "the unpleasantness . . . when each swallow was punctuated with bombs going off on the Prado or the sound of . . . shells being fired at the Hotel Nacional."

Our specs for the drink are as follows. It is one that we continually serve not just because we live in the state that is the namesake of the USS *Maine* but because it's a drink that we truly love: whiskey and sweet vermouth, textured with a bit of cherry liqueur and an absinthe rinse. It's a classic drink that you don't have to be in Maine to love.

YIELD: 1 DRINK ⚓ GLASS: CHILLED COCKTAIL

2 ounces rye whiskey (we use Old Overholt)

¾ ounce sweet vermouth

2 teaspoons Cherry Heering

3 pumps absinthe from an atomizer (see page 17)

Cocktail cherry, for garnish

Combine the whiskey, sweet vermouth, Cherry Heering, and absinthe in a mixing glass.

Add ice to fill the glass, and then stir for 20 to 30 seconds.

Strain into a chilled cocktail glass and garnish with the cherry.

SMOKE + BITTERS

Our bar manager, Trey Hughes, took a very nontraditional path to bartending and bar management. He started out as a professional musician working in a guitar store (for the equipment discounts, of course). He grew up in North Carolina and found his way to Portland, Oregon, before anyone cool was living there. Trey and his wife eventually moved to Maine, where they settled about thirty minutes north of Portland to raise their two children.

Years later, Trey started picking up cocktail books and sourcing obscure ingredients to make his own amari and shrubs, mixing up cocktails for himself and his wife in the evenings. Eventually, Trey parlayed his knowledge and personality into running the tiniest bar imaginable at a small restaurant on Portland's Munjoy Hill. There were three seats at the bar, a camp cooler with ice, and room for fewer than twenty bottles. Trey killed it. When we moved back to Portland and started to see what was going on in the bar scene, so many people told us we had to meet Trey. When we did, we hit it off immediately. He joined us as part of the opening team at Hunt + Alpine, and this was one of his first drinks to hit the menu.

Smoke + Bitters is a cocktail that shouldn't taste as amazing as it does. On paper, mezcal, Fernet-Branca, Cynar, and tequila appear to be competing flavors that don't play well together. However, when they are mixed together with ice and the grapefruit twist is layered on, the result is delicious. In fact, it is one of our all-time favorite mezcal cocktails. When you're ready to expand your home bar with these spirits, this is the first drink you need to make.

YIELD: 1 DRINK ⚜ GLASS: CHILLED COCKTAIL

---

1 ounce tequila

1 ounce Cynar

½ ounce mezcal

½ ounce Fernet-Branca

Grapefruit peel, for garnish

Combine the tequila, Cynar, mezcal, and Fernet-Branca in a mixing glass.

Add ice to fill the glass, and then stir for 20 to 30 seconds.

Strain into a chilled cocktail glass and garnish with a grapefruit peel.

CHAPTER 3

COCKTAILS FOR A CROWD

LET'S GET THIS PARTY STARTED!

Hunt + Alpine was made for crowds. We have a bar that seats fifteen people, with corners and tight spaces that encourage our guests to be elbow-to-elbow with their neighbors. Our main seating is two large communal tables; they are great for big groups and encourage strangers to become friends. Our private event space, the Lodge Room, was designed to bring groups together—the cozy, sauna-like space has hosted many a birthday and bachelor or bachelorette party.

Even before we opened the bar, we loved entertaining and hosting all types of gatherings. We've hosted big, messy ragers where the night didn't end until someone was lying on our dining table with a new friend pouring Chartreuse into their mouth (yes, this happened). We've also hosted mellow, secret, invite-only cocktail hours in our former apartment, turning it into a sort of speakeasy. This experience, plus over a dozen years behind the bar, has taught us that we can't do everything in the moment and still have fun. That's where advance preparation comes in. When done correctly, you get drinks in your guests' hands, and more importantly, you stay sane and enjoy the party too. Before you write it off, this doesn't mean you need to serve your grandma's punch with sherbet ice rings or put out college-style bowls of trashcan punch (though there's nothing wrong with that, depending on the occasion). We're talking classics such as an Old Fashioned, just pre-batched so all you need to do is add ice and a garnish. Likewise, what's so wrong about pitchers full of Sloe Gin Fizz? Frankly, a punch is a welcome addition to any party, as long as you're doing it right, with fresh juice, quality spirits, and a giant ice block.

At Hunt + Alpine, this advance preparation takes on a few different forms; we have one drink on tap and a punch that changes daily based on the bartender's mood. At home, we don't put drinks on tap, but we do make sure that drinks are easy to assemble, pour, or serve so we aren't wasting time mixing drinks when we would rather be spending time with our friends. It's very easy to keep a couple of empty, clean wine bottles on hand to prepare cocktails ahead of time. Pouring pre-batched drinks straight from a bottle keeps the conversation flowing—when you're serving low-alcohol cocktails, it lets guests serve themselves at dinner just like they would with wine.

PUNCH

When you have a seat at the bar at Hunt + Alpine, you may notice a large bowl of punch sitting on our backbar. We make a fresh bowl daily, with the recipe based partly on the weather and partly on the opening bartender's whim. With something like punch, the conversation is so much more than a single recipe. Entire books can be written on punch as a form of drinking, entertainment, and celebration. In fact, our friend David Wondrich has written such a book on the history of punch, appropriately called *Punch*. (Go read it.)

Presented below is one of our favorite basic formulas for punch. It can be modified and scaled up or down, you can replace the sweet ingredient with a different one, or you can switch out the bourbon with another spirit you have on hand. Perhaps you have fresh grapefruit and limes? Use those instead of the lemon, and pair with tequila or gin. Or if it's cold out, make this a hot punch by omitting the ice and adding more hot water. Even better for a cold night, split the bourbon into two parts Scotch and one part cognac for a more robust flavor. The possibilities are truly endless. Play with it and you'll quickly develop some of your own house favorites.

**YIELD: APPROXIMATELY 4 CUPS BEFORE ICE DILUTION, CAN BE SCALED
(ENOUGH FOR A ROUND OF DRINKS FOR A SMALL GROUP)**

2 lemons

½ cup sugar

1 tea bag, black

½ cup hot water

10 ounces 100-proof bourbon

Ice block (see page 48)

16 ounces soda water, or to taste

Peel the lemons and place the peels in a heatproof container, such as a small glass mixing bowl or large glass measuring cup. Mix in the sugar. Let the peels rest in the sugar for at least 1 hour and up to 4 hours, occasionally stirring and pressing to release the oils from the lemon peels.

Meanwhile, squeeze the lemons and set aside the juice.

When the lemon oil has been extracted from the peels and is infused into the sugar, you're ready to move on to the next step.

In a ceramic cup or very small heatproof bowl, steep the tea bag in ½ cup hot water for 6 minutes. Remove the tea bag from the water and pour the hot tea into the bowl with the lemon peel and sugar mixture. Stir well enough to dissolve all the sugar. Add the bourbon and lemon juice to the bowl and stir to combine.

Place the ice block in a serving bowl. Slowly pour the punch over the ice block and stir to chill. You can strain out the lemon peels or leave them in depending on your preference.

Add the soda water to dilute the punch to taste.

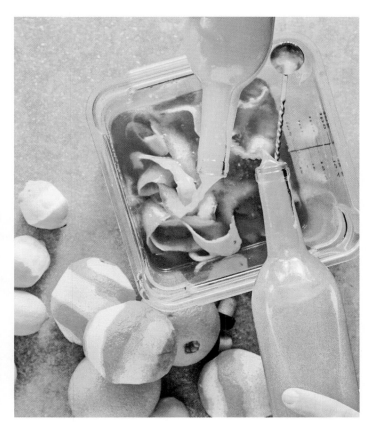

THE IMPORTANCE OF RAD ICE

Even though ice is something that we're all very familiar with (especially in Maine), there is an immense fascination with ice among bartenders. This can mean a number of different things depending on your level of commitment, the time you have, and what drinks you are serving.

Let's start with the easiest, and yet still impressive, step to upping your ice game: silicone molds. There are a number of companies currently producing nearly any shape. We love the 2-inch cubes, and they fit very nicely in nearly any large old fashioned glass; some folks love the spherical molds as well. Both the spheres and large cubes have an important function besides looking cool: they have reduced surface area compared to a bunch of little cubes, so they melt into your drink more slowly. This keeps your drink at the perfect temperature and dilution level longer, before it gets too watery. Additionally, if you find yourself with a surplus of large cubes, they are wonderful to shake your cocktails with (see page 6), as they add a velvety texture to a shaken drink.

Once you start using large ice cube trays, you may find yourself chasing a pristinely clear ice cube, one without any blemishes or traces of air trapped inside. There have been numerous papers, articles, and conference presentations on how to achieve this feat—and there are (very expensive) machines that make perfectly clear 300-pound blocks of ice. However, it is something that you can achieve at home.

There are two major factors that contribute to blemishes in the freezing process: impurities in your water and the way water freezes. Impurities in your water can be anything from microorganisms to minerals; you want to make sure you're using filtered, distilled, or otherwise extra-pure water. Depending on where you draw water from, it's a good bet that you may have to buy water for this. The other factor to getting a blemish-free cube is controlling the direction in which the ice freezes. A traditional ice cube tray is uninsulated on all sides, which means that the water freezes on all exterior surfaces at the same time and freezes inward. Typically, water molecules will create a perfectly clear lattice as the temperature drops, but as you're creating six different lattices (one on each side of a cube), those six will have to join together in the middle of the ice cube, which traps air and imperfections at the center. Instead, you can control the number of surfaces with directional freezing. There are commercial trays out there that are insulated on all sides but the top, or there are some in-home hacks (such as putting ice trays in a small cooler in your freezer), but the purpose of each is to allow the cubes to only freeze in one direction instead of six. If all else fails, you may be able to purchase ice from a professional supplier in your city. Regardless of your chosen method, your guests are going to be seriously impressed with crystal-clear cubes of ice in their drinks.

Another impressive ice preparation method is to make a large block of ice for a bowl of punch. This requires just a little bit of forethought and planning, but it can look incredible with a bit of practice. First, determine the bowl that the punch will be served in and find a bowl or other container just a bit smaller to use as your ice mold. Fill the smaller bowl three-quarters of the way with water, and freeze it overnight. Just before your guests arrive, remove the ice block from the freezer and separate the block from its mold by running some room-temperature water over the bottom of the bowl. Place the ice in the punch bowl and fill the bowl with your punch. The large block not only looks good, but it melts much slower than lots of smaller cubes of ice, keeping your punch strong and cool for a much longer period of time.

It is easy to take an ice block to the next level by adding a complementary color (if you're making a red punch, think about adding blue curaçao or food coloring to the water before freezing) or by placing thin slices of fruit at the bottom of your mold before adding water. When you remove the block the next day, your fruit will be suspended in the ice block, and your punch will look even more impressive.

WHITE NOISE

This is one of our most popular drinks. It has been on the menu without a break since we opened, and it is a drink that we are incredibly proud of. It's simple yet pleases many different types of guests on multiple levels. First and foremost, it's so delicious that almost everyone enjoys it. Slightly sweet without being syrupy, it's a perfect drink to sip while deciding on dinner. It uses Cocchi Americano Bianco, a product imported from Italy that uses wine as its base. The wine is fortified, sweetened, and aromatized, leaving a pleasing play between sweetness and bitterness on the tongue. (It is an ingredient that even the geekiest cocktailian would be happy to serve a crowd.) Our staff loves this drink because it's very simple to make round after round (and they do get ordered by the table), so you'll find it is a very easy drink to batch at home for a party as well. Finally, this drink is great because it's low in alcohol; it is a great spacer when you feel like you don't want something strong, and it's wonderful to sip all night long when you're just not in the mood for stronger spirits.

YIELD: 1 DRINK, CAN BE SCALED (WE MAKE 5-GALLON KEGS OF THIS DRINK AT THE RESTAURANT) ⚗ **GLASS: CHILLED DOUBLE OLD FASHIONED**

1½ ounces Cocchi Americano Bianco

1 ounce elderflower liqueur

2 ounces soda water

Grapefruit twist, for garnish

In a chilled double old fashioned glass, combine the Cocchi Americano Bianco and the elderflower liqueur.

Fill the glass with ice, and then top with the soda water. Stir gently to incorporate, and garnish with an expressed grapefruit twist.

WHITE NOISE (PITCHER RECIPE)
YIELD: 64-OUNCE PITCHER (6 DRINKS, WITH ICE)

9 ounces Cocchi Americano Bianco

6 ounces elderflower liqueur

12 ounces soda water

Grapefruit twists, for garnish

Pour the Cocchi Americano Bianco and elderflower liqueur into a pitcher.

Fill the pitcher with ice, then top with the soda water.

Stir gently to incorporate, and garnish with several grapefruit twists. To serve, pour gently from the pitcher, making sure to spoon in some ice along with the liquid. Do not allow the drink to sit too long before serving, as the ice will melt and dilute it.

A BARTENDER'S GUIDE TO HOSTING A CROWD

Prep, prep, and more prep! So much of a bartender's job is in the preparation, which is essential to successfully hosting a group of people. Professional bartenders have speed wells, pre-juiced fruit, and entire cockpits geared towards efficiency at their disposal to make their jobs as smooth and comfortable as possible. This allows bartenders to focus on their guests, making sure they are taken care of beyond just cocktails. Here are a few other ideas for elevating your hosting game at the home bar.

Start by keeping things simple. Don't complicate the night by giving yourself too much to take on. It's far more impressive to quickly put together a well-executed but simple cocktail than to spend thirty minutes making five complicated drinks. If you've hosted a dinner party before, you may have already learned this lesson with food; now apply it to drinks as well.

Practice before your guests arrive to make sure you are comfortable with what you're doing. You can always tell if a bartender is uncomfortable or in the weeds if their head is down and they aren't engaging the people around them. The same is true at home. Remember that you have a full party in front of you, so get out from behind the bar (or the kitchen) and spend time with people. If you're not having fun and enjoying the party, what's the point?

There are other ways to impress your guests outside of the drinks you serve. Try to think up a few small things that make an impact. Printed and personalized menus, donuts for the drive home, or rad ice (see page 48) are the little, thoughtful details that your guests will remember. Long before Briana worked in restaurants professionally, she worked with bands and musicians to put together events and afterparties for concerts. At one such event, when she was working the door for the Roots, she was asked to fetch dozens of donuts as the guests left. She was reluctant, thinking it was a bogus idea. However, as everything wound down and guests started leaving, when they were given donuts, they were floored beyond belief. The short of it is that the memory of one unexpected treat will last a long time—and likely be just as killer as whatever you served.

We looooooove the opportunities presented by large-format options. We're talking about magnums of wine, overflowing bowls of punch, and smorgasbords that fill whole tables. Get into large-format drinks and eats! Not only does it allow you to prep more before and fuss less during your party; sharing from the same plate or bottle brings a social and visceral aspect to your soiree. Who isn't happy when a 15-liter Nebuchadnezzar of bubbly is placed on the table?

MEXICAN TRIKE

This drink is an example of how recipes can evolve over time and through different bartenders' hands. At its origin, this drink was the Italian classic Bicicletta, which combines Campari, white wine, and soda water into a refreshing, afternoon aperitif–style drink. Working at Clyde Common in Portland, Oregon, our good friend Jeff Morgenthaler developed his Broken Bike, which substituted the darker, savory Cynar for Campari. Taking inspiration from this (with an ancillary and short-lived step of a Cynar and Cocchi Americano drink we called the Trike), at Hunt + Alpine we were searching for drinks to round out our autumn menu. We decided to mix Cynar and cider in a way similar to how it was used in Jeff's imagining of the drink. When it fell a bit flat on its own, the addition of mezcal punched up the flavor and added a depth to the drink without overtaking the flavors.

YIELD: 1 DRINK, CAN BE SCALED ⊛ GLASS: COLLINS

1 ounce Cynar

1 ounce mezcal

4 ounces hard cider (we use Bantam's Wunderkind cider, but any mild and not-too-sweet cider will do)

Lemon twist, for garnish

In a Collins glass, combine the Cynar and mezcal. Fill the glass with ice, and then top with the hard cider. Stir briefly and garnish with a lemon twist.

MEXICAN TRIKE (PITCHER RECIPE)
YIELD: 64-OUNCE PITCHER (6 DRINKS, WITH ICE)

6 ounces Cynar

6 ounces mezcal

24 ounces hard cider

Lemon twist, for garnish

Pour the Cynar and mezcal into the pitcher. Fill the pitcher with ice, and then top with the hard cider. Stir gently to incorporate, and garnish with several lemon twists.

Pour gently into guests' glasses when ready to serve, making sure to spoon over some ice as well. Do not allow the drink to sit too long, as the ice will melt and dilute it.

LION'S TAIL

This cocktail dates back to the Prohibition era and utilizes allspice dram, an ingredient that was popular in the 1920s and 1930s but then unavailable until the early 2000s. Allspice dram is an intensely savory and herbaceous liqueur. If you can't find allspice dram (we use St. Elizabeth's), you can substitute the Hunt + Alpine Cardamom-Coriander Syrup (see page 74).

A variation on a bourbon sour, the recipe allows the host to prepare a pitcher or bottle of this drink before a party. Scale the recipe to the size of the container you have or the number of guests you are expecting. We've included a recipe for one drink as well as a batched size that will fill an empty wine bottle. Then when a guest is ready for a drink, you can simply eye-ball the amount needed, pour it into a mixing tin, add ice, and shake—the drink is going to turn out perfect every time.

YIELD: 1 DRINK ❖ GLASS: CHILLED COCKTAIL

2 ounces bourbon

¾ ounce fresh lime juice

¼ ounce allspice dram

¼ ounce rich simple syrup (see page 191)

1 dash Angostura bitters

Combine the bourbon, lime juice, allspice dram, syrup, and bitters in a mixing tin.

Fill the tin with ice, cap, and shake hard for 20 seconds.

Fine strain the drink into a chilled cocktail glass and serve.

LION'S TAIL (BATCHED RECIPE)
YIELD: 7 TO 10 DRINKS, DEPENDING ON PORTIONING AND GLASSWARE SIZE

14 ounces bourbon

5¼ ounces fresh lime juice

1¾ ounces allspice dram

1¾ ounces rich simple syrup (see page 191)

7 dashes Angostura bitters

Combine the bourbon, lime juice, allspice dram, syrup, and bitters in a large vessel, such as a 4-cup measuring cup. Stir gently to incorporate, and then strain into an empty, clean 750ml wine bottle.

When you're ready to serve a drink, gently agitate the bottle to ensure equal distribution of all ingredients.

Pour enough for the desired number of drinks into a mixing tin. Fill the tin with ice, cap, and shake hard for 20 seconds.

Fine strain the drink(s) into chilled cocktail glasses.

THE RULES OF BATCHING

The most important thing to remember about batching is to keep it simple. Your guests are going to be the most impressed when you're able to keep a level head while making drinks, serving food, introducing them to each other, and acting the part of host. They're going to remember the great party more than they remember the sixteen bittering agents that went into your housemade bitters.

When you're scaling a recipe up from something that makes one to something that serves many more, it is often not as simple as multiplying all of the ingredients by the number of servings. Ingredients that bring alcohol (spirits), acid (juice), or sugar (syrups and some liqueurs) can be multiplied. However, anything that is adding bittering levels or depth of flavor (bitters, digestifs) is usually more potent in large batches than it is in a single drink, while the balance of acid and sugar can be skewed in large quantities. For these reasons, when scaling a drink at home we recommend building slowly. First make the drink with the spirit and acid (juice) components multiplied out from one recipe to the number of recipes you hope to achieve. From there, add 60 percent of the amount of sweet ingredients that would be required, and keep tasting until the sweet and acid are balanced together. You can pull a small amount and shake it with ice or train your palate to discern balance without dilution—it's all about practice! Continue to add sugar until the drink is in balance. Finally, do the same thing with about 50 percent of the amount of bittering agents you would use if you scaled up by the numbers. Add that first 50 percent, make a test drink, and slowly add bitters until the drink tastes the same as what a single-service recipe would produce.

Remember, you can always add more bitters or sugar, but it's very difficult to remove or recover when too much is added.

BATCHING STRATEGY

When planning a party where you are going to batch cocktails, first congratulate yourself. You're doing the smart thing! Second, think about what you're serving, who your guests are, and how the drinks are going to be served.

If you're making a lighter fare or putting out small bites, perhaps keep the drink options to something lower in alcohol (see White Noise, page 51). Alternatively, if you're providing a full meal with steak, have a bottle of Manhattans ready to stir up as the steaks are resting. Think about who will be attending your party, and make sure to accommodate them in the drinks selection, as with everything else. Is your "vodka-only" mother coming? Make sure she has something to drink and that you're not just pouring her brown, bitter, and stirred drinks all night.

Importantly, and perhaps most over-looked, think about how your guests will be served their drinks. This doesn't just mean the glassware, though that is important. Will your guests be serving themselves from a punch bowl, or will you be shaking up a batched bottle of Lion's Tails (see page 57) for them?

Once you have planned what you will be serving, prepping and timing your drinks will be easy. Any spirituous ingredients can be combined days ahead of your party. Fruit should be juiced the day of, but several hours before anyone arrives is perfectly acceptable—and you can get away with doing it the day before if you're immediately mixing it with alcohol. Mix sugar syrups the day before and keep them in the refrigerator. Garnishes should be prepared at the last minute so they're at their best.

SLOE GIN FIZZ

This is a great daytime or brunch drink and a good way to start a day of sitting on the porch in the sun with friends. Historically "fizzes" as a category were served in very short glasses (think old-school juice glasses) with a shot of soda water but no ice. They were meant to be consumed quickly and without much consideration. We've always chosen to respect that and encourage you to try it out as well.

YIELD: 1 DRINK ❧ GLASS: CHILLED SINGLE OLD FASHIONED

2 ounces sloe gin (use the best you can find—we enjoy Plymouth)

1 ounce fresh lemon juice

½ ounce rich simple syrup (see page 191)

2 ounces soda water

Lemon peel, for garnish

Combine the sloe gin, lemon juice, and syrup in a mixing tin.

Fill the tin with ice, cap, and shake hard for 20 seconds.

Fine strain into a chilled single old fashioned glass with no ice. Add the soda water and lemon peel and drink quickly!

SLOE GIN FIZZ (PITCHER RECIPE)

"Portland, Oregon, and Sloe Gin Fizz. If that ain't love, then tell me what is." —Loretta Lynn

YIELD: 64-OUNCE PITCHER, CAN BE SCALED TO YOUR PREFERRED VESSEL SIZE

12 ounces sloe gin

6 ounces fresh lemon juice

3 ounces rich simple syrup

12 ounces soda water

Lemon peels, for garnish

Combine sloe gin, lemon juice, syrup, and soda water in a pitcher, and then add ice to fill.

Stir gently to incorporate. Pour into individual chilled glasses, straining so that no ice goes into the glasses. If you want, you can use a little extra soda water to top up any flat drinks. Garnish each with a lemon peel. Drink quickly!

HUNT + ALPINE
OLD FASHIONED

Eight years ago, a girl walked into a bar and ordered an Old Fashioned. Little did she or the bartender know that it would be the beginning of something very big for them.

Whether you know it at the time or not, there are drinks that can change the trajectory of your life. The Old Fashioned was that drink for us. We met, talked, and fell in love over Old Fashioneds—and now have shared more than we can count. One of the most classic cocktails, which has undoubtedly launched a million love affairs, it has been on the Hunt + Alpine menu since day one. We think we've perfected the recipe, creating a spirit-forward but balanced version that doesn't veer far from any classic recipe you've seen. It's also an incredibly easy drink to make for a crowd. Win, win.

YIELD: 1 DRINK　　GLASS: CHILLED DOUBLE OLD FASHIONED

---

2 ounces whiskey (we like Old Grand-Dad Bonded)

1 teaspoon rich simple syrup (see page 191)

2 dashes Angostura bitters

Cocktail cherry and orange peel, for garnish

Combine the whiskey, syrup, and bitters in a chilled double old fashioned glass. Add ice and stir. Add the cherry, express the orange peel over the glass, and serve.

HUNT + ALPINE OLD FASHIONED (BATCHED VERSION)
YIELD: 8-12 DRINKS, DEPENDING ON GLASSWARE AND HOW HEAVY YOU POUR

---

18 ounces whiskey (we like Old Grand-Dad Bonded)

1½ ounces rich simple syrup (see page 191)

12 dashes Angostura bitters, or to taste

Cocktail cherries and orange peels, for garnish

This drink recipe can be multiplied as shown here (or to a different batch size) and poured into many glasses, without ice, before your guests arrive. When you're ready to serve a guest, simply place ice into the glass, give it a stir, and add a garnish.

Alternatively, the recipe can be scaled and batched into a clean and empty 750ml bottle. Mix everything together but the garnishes, and funnel into a clean wine bottle. Chill until ready to serve. When serving, put a pour spout into the bottle and place the bottle alongside a bucket of ice, glassware, a couple of oranges, a peeler for the oranges, and a cup of cherries.

SMOKED TROUT DEVILED EGGS

Deviled eggs have been one of our favorite party snacks for years, and we've encountered innumerable variations on them. When we opened Hunt + Alpine, we knew we wanted an upscale Scandinavian version of the classic. We have a great relationship with a fish purveyor less than a mile down the road. They smoke their own trout, among other fish, and we knew immediately that we wanted to use that in our deviled eggs. Over the years, we've departed from just offering the smoked trout deviled eggs and now have a rotating selection of equally delicious options, but these still hold a special place in our heart, and we're always happy to eat a couple of these with a cocktail.

YIELD: 24 PIECES

1 pound smoked trout

½ cup finely diced shallots

1 cup crème fraîche

1 tablespoon chopped fresh dill

1 tablespoon chopped fresh chives

1 tablespoon chopped fresh parsley

1 tablespoon chopped fresh cilantro

2 lemons, zested

½ teaspoon white pepper

1 tablespoon fresh lemon juice, or to taste

1 teaspoon salt, or to taste

1 dozen eggs

Clean the skin (if you've purchased a side of smoked trout) and shred the smoked trout.

Combine the shredded trout, shallots, crème fraîche, dill, chives, parsley, cilantro, lemon zest, white pepper, lemon juice, and salt in a mixing bowl and stir gently to combine. Cover and set aside in the refrigerator while continuing with the recipe.

Bring a pot of water to a boil. There should be enough water to cover the eggs once they are placed in the pot. Once the water reaches a boil, carefully add the eggs and reduce the heat to a simmer. Cook the eggs for 11 minutes. After 11 minutes, remove the eggs and immediately transfer them to an ice bath to stop the cooking.

Peel the eggs under running water, then slice each egg in half lengthwise. Remove the yolks and fill the empty egg whites with the smoked trout filling.

Our favorite way to serve these is to spread Brown-Butter Mayonnaise on a serving plate, place the eggs on top, then shave the leftover egg yolks over the top and sprinkle our Pickled Red Onions (see page 114) over the whole plate. Feel free to experiment!

DILL POTATO SALAD

Potato salad may seem like the low-hanging fruit when it comes to eats for a large crowd, but that doesn't make it any less delicious. We think this recipe, a marriage of traditional potato salad and mashed potatoes, complements almost any spread, no matter the season. It can be served hot or cold as well, which gives you many pairing options. And, of course, it's a perfect accompaniment to drinking.

YIELD: 4 TO 6 SERVINGS AS A SIDE

1 pound fingerling or new potatoes

½ cup sour cream

½ cup mayonnaise (we like Hellmann's or Best Foods)

Kewpie mayonnaise, to taste

1 large bunch fresh dill, chopped

1 tablespoon salt

In a large pot, bring 5 quarts of water to a rolling boil. Season with 1 tablespoon of salt. Once the water comes to a boil, carefully place the potatoes in the water and boil for 15 minutes.

Check the potatoes for doneness with a fork; if it can easily be inserted, then they are done. Drain the potatoes and transfer them to a large mixing bowl.

With a fork or pastry blender, press the potatoes against the side of the bowl to smash them. Let them remain somewhat intact and aim for a chunky mash.

Once the potatoes are about as mashed as you'd like, add the sour cream, mayonnaise, and two-thirds of the dill. Mix thoroughly, and add salt and pepper to taste.

NOTE: *This is the point where you'd add Kewpie mayonnaise if you'd like. We suggest starting with a couple of tablespoons. Alternately, you can replace ¼ cup regular mayonnaise with the Kewpie for a richer dressing.*

If serving warm, transfer to a serving bowl and garnish with the remaining chopped dill. If serving cold, refrigerate, covered, for at least 2 hours. When you're ready to serve, garnish with the remaining dill and optionally some dried, crushed spices, such as Aleppo red pepper or a turn of black pepper.

OVEN PANCAKES

Oven pancakes are one of those simple dishes that never get old. Just like with their more popular cousins, pies and galettes, you can use fresh fruit or berries to change the recipe by season. They're also easy to scale, and they make a wonderful brunch dish for a few friends or a big family gathering. Since the pancake itself is a fairly neutral base, you can add almost anything to it. If you want to keep it incredibly simple, go with a dusting of powdered sugar and a drizzle of honey. Being Mainers, we'd be remiss to not suggest warm maple syrup.

YIELD: 4 TO 6 SERVINGS

2 cups cake flour (all-purpose flour can be substituted)

1 teaspoon salt

4 eggs, at room temperature

4½ cups whole milk

4 tablespoons unsalted or cultured butter

1 cup fresh fruit, such as blueberries, apricots, plums, or raspberries (optional)

Powdered sugar, warm maple syrup, honey butter, or jam, for garnish (optional)

Preheat your oven to 425°F.

Combine the flour and salt together in a large bowl. In a separate bowl, whisk together the eggs and milk.

Slowly add the wet mixture to the flour, and fold in. Mix gently as you add the wet mixture; it's okay to have a few lumps in the batter.

Add the butter to a large cast-iron skillet and place the skillet in the hot oven. Once the butter has melted but before it browns, remove the skillet from the oven and pour the batter into the skillet. Sprinkle the fresh fruit, if using, over the top of the batter.

Return the skillet to the oven and cook the pancake until a knife comes out clean from the center, about 25 minutes.

Once the pancake is done, you can remove it and let it cool on a wire rack, or you can let it cool in the skillet. (Just be aware that if it cools in the cast iron, it will continue to cook as the pan retains some heat.)

Either in the pan or on a large plate, garnish the pancake with powdered sugar, warm maple syrup, honey butter, or jam, if desired. Alternatively, you can serve the pancake plain and let your guests garnish their own slices once they're served.

Winters in Maine are long—very long—which means Mainers are wonderful at making the most of the dark, cold time of year. We have learned to embrace winter and enjoy the outdoors; from ice fishing and skiing to snowy walks on the beach, being outside is crucial to our way of life. When we come in from the cold, we need ways to warm ourselves, our friends, and our family. After a long day snowshoeing, gathering around a blazing fire with drinks and food warms you right to your bones. Being in a room full of people and seeing rosy-cheeked friends peeling off the layers from the day as they get cozy in your home is one of the great joys of winter.

WHY WE LOVE WARM COCKTAILS

Since fire and alcohol have been around, warm drinks have been keeping us cozy. Warm cocktails get to the heart of it; warming the drinkers up quickly helps us forget about the elements outside. Warm drinks immediately make anyone feel welcome, no matter where they are. Cocktails can provide the perfect transition between the cold outside and the warmth of a home or bar.

All winter long, we have a section of the Hunt + Alpine menu dedicated to warm cocktails. From a non-greasy version of a hot buttered rum (helllllllo, ice cream!) to a hot toddy that uses one of Finland's favorite baking spices, we can't think of a better way to warm us all. We've also brought Spanish Coffee to the East Coast. (Don't let the name fool you—the rich drink has its roots deeply planted in the Pacific Northwest, not Spain.)

We would be remiss to not mention a wintertime staple in Maine, Allen's Coffee Brandy. (Actually, if we are being honest, Maine's love of Allen's is not limited to the snowy months.) If you're unfamiliar, Allen's Coffee Brandy is a coffee liqueur that became popular among fisherman, many of whom would add a splash to their morning coffees as they motored out to their lobster traps. It is the unofficial drink of Maine, easily outselling any other brand of spirits. Though popular among fishermen for decades, it has slowly become more popular in cocktail circles in recent years (because it's delicious). The most commonly seen combination is Allen's and milk, a drink with varying nicknames depending on where you are in the state (none of them printable). In fact, Allen's Coffee Brandy is so prevalent here in Maine that empty bottles found in the spring along snowmobile trails are called "Lilies of the Tundra." It's the only coffee liqueur we use at Hunt + Alpine and at home.

ANTHOLOGY CLUB

We're often asked where we get inspiration for the names of drinks. The truth is that it can come from nearly anywhere. We keep a list of potential cocktail names so when we develop a drink in need of one we're ready. That's just what happened for the Anthology Club, which is what we ended up calling our cognac riff on a Negroni. With the addition of a cardamom syrup that we make in the winter months, this drink is a spectacular winter warmer. It's strong, silky, and smooth, and it warms you immediately and keeps you coming back for more.

What is the Anthology Club? When you delve deep into the intersections of cocktail history and New England history, the family name Tudor arises. In 1806, well before refrigeration, Frederic Tudor and his brother William shipped a vessel of block ice from their family's farm in Saugus, Massachusetts, to the Caribbean island of Martinique. This trip was the first of many that Frederic made to earn himself the nickname "Ice King." William, on the other hand, found the manual labor required too difficult and instead focused on literary pursuits. He went on to become one of the founding members of Boston's Anthology Club, a literary society that became one of the oldest independent libraries in the United States.

YIELD: 1 DRINK ⤍ **GLASS: CHILLED COCKTAIL**

---

1 ounce cognac (we use Pierre Ferrand 1840 cognac)

1 ounce sweet vermouth (we use Punt e Mes)

1 ounce Campari

1 teaspoon Hunt + Alpine Cardamom-Coriander Syrup (recipe follows)

Orange twist, for garnish

Combine the cognac, vermouth, Campari, and syrup in a mixing glass. Add enough ice to fill the glass.

Stir for 20 to 30 seconds, and then strain into a chilled cocktail glass. Garnish with an orange twist and serve.

HUNT + ALPINE
CARDAMOM-CORIANDER SYRUP

As cocktails slowly made their comeback over the past twenty years, bartenders often found recipes requiring ingredients that weren't commercially available. For many years, one of those ingredients was allspice dram, a strong and unique blend of allspice, cloves, rum, and other spices. Before it was available in Maine, we often blended our own allspice dram to use in classics such as the Lion's Tail (see page 57) or in numerous tiki drinks. This recipe came about because we wanted to create a similar mixture that highlighted flavors familiar to the Scandinavian palate. One of our go-to spices in these instances is black cardamom, a relative of the more common green cardamom, which has a savory and smoky flavor. Black cardamom is most often used in Asian cuisines, but it found its way into Scandinavian countries and cuisine, along with many other exotic spices, through trade. Cardamom is featured prominently in Finnish baked treats, including pulla (see page 170).

YIELD: APPROXIMATELY 24 OUNCES

- **2 cinnamon sticks, broken up**
- **1½ teaspoons coriander seeds**
- **1 tablespoon black cardamom pods, roughly broken (do not use green cardamom)**
- **¼ teaspoon red pepper flakes**
- **4 ounces high-proof rum**
- **15 ounces hot water**
- **¾ cup fine granulated sugar**

Preheat the oven to 450°F.

Spread the cinnamon sticks, coriander seeds, and cardamom on a rimmed baking sheet and toast in the oven, tossing occasionally to prevent burning, until fragrant but not burned, about 8 minutes.

Combine the toasted spices, red pepper flakes, and rum in a blender, and blend on high speed until evenly ground, about 2 minutes.

Meanwhile, in a separate container, combine the hot water and sugar, and stir until the sugar is completely dissolved. Set aside.

Using a coffee filter or multiple layers of cheesecloth, strain the spice and rum mixture into the sugar syrup. Stir to combine. Transfer to a clean, sealable bottle or container.

This syrup will keep, refrigerated, for 2 months. Shake thoroughly before using.

SPIRIT-FORWARD EQUAL-PARTS COCKTAILS

Not every drink meant to warm you up must itself be warm. Spirit-forward cocktails are a go-to option when we're not in the mood for something hot. Equal-parts cocktails are a fine choice not only due to their warming quality, but also because of their simplicity; they're easy to remember, easy to reproduce, and easy to throw together at a moment's notice.

The spirit-forward equal-parts cocktail that most people are familiar with is the Negroni, thanks in large part to the resurgence of attention focused on bartenders and cocktail bars over the past twenty years. Typically, a spirit-forward equal-parts cocktail contains three parts, so we will use the Negroni as an example: use one ounce of something strong (gin), one ounce of something sweet (vermouth), and one ounce of something bitter (Campari).

This is a wonderful template to use as a base for creating new drinks. With some basic knowledge of ingredients, you can quickly and easily create a drink that works with your favorite flavors or simply with what you have sitting on your home bar. For instance, if you drop the gin in a Negroni and replace it with whiskey, you have a Boulevardier. And as you may have noticed, the Anthology Club on page 73 is also an equal-parts cocktail. The combination of a rich, aged cognac such as Pierre Ferrand's 1840 with vermouth and Campari makes up its base, though we do punch it up with a kick of warming cardamom. Want to give another equal-parts cocktail a try? Here are a few classic recipes to get you started.

NEGRONI

This drink is an Italian classic that has, thankfully, become a modern American classic as of late. For the home bartender, this is one of the first and easiest drinks to learn. It's a wonderful predinner, with dinner, or after-dinner drink. It's equally acceptable to make this up or on the rocks. Additionally, you can adjust the flavors quite a bit in this drink, depending on the gin or sweet vermouth you choose.

YIELD: 1 DRINK ⁓ **GLASS: CHILLED COCKTAIL OR DOUBLE OLD FASHIONED**

1 ounce gin

1 ounce Campari

1 ounce sweet vermouth

Orange twist, for garnish

Combine the gin, Campari, and vermouth in a mixing glass with ice. Stir for 30 to 45 seconds, until well chilled. Pour into a chilled cocktail glass or over ice in a chilled double old fashioned glass. Garnish with an orange twist.

BOULEVARDIER

A rye whiskey version of a Negroni, a Boulevardier has the balance of a Negroni while bringing the weight of whiskey along too.

YIELD: 1 DRINK   **GLASS: CHILLED COCKTAIL**

1 ounce rye whiskey

1 ounce Campari

1 ounce sweet vermouth

Lemon twist, for garnish

Combine the whiskey, Campari, and vermouth in a mixing glass with ice. Stir for 30 to 45 seconds, until well chilled. Pour into a chilled cocktail glass. Garnish with a lemon twist.

WHITE NEGRONI

A White Negroni is a summery, lighter version of the Italian classic. At Hunt + Alpine, we really enjoy the subtlety and softness that Cocchi Americano Bianco brings, along with a sweeter, bolder Old Tom–style gin.

YIELD: 1 DRINK   **GLASS: CHILLED COCKTAIL**

1 ounce Old Tom–style gin (we use Tanqueray's limited release; Hayman's is widely available)

1 ounce Cocchi Americano Bianco

1 ounce blanc-style vermouth (Dolin works great here)

Grapefruit twist, for garnish

Combine the gin, Cocchi American Bianco, and vermouth in a mixing glass with ice. Stir for 30 to 45 seconds, until well chilled. Pour into a chilled cocktail glass. Garnish with a grapefruit twist.

HOT TODDY

On particularly cold evenings, we keep glasses preheated and ready to go for this wintertime classic. You'll find our version keeps the recipe straightforward, allowing our guests to choose whether they want brandy, for a slightly fruitier and mellow drink, or bourbon, for a stronger and more bracing drink. Using fresh ginger syrup adds a zip that can help knock out a cold (so they say), and the cardamom-coriander syrup brings a depth of flavor that many hot toddies lack. The slightly complex setup while mixing ensures the drink reaches you and your guests at the ideal temperature (hot!) and not tepid, as is too often the case.

YIELD: 1 DRINK ✌ **GLASS: GLASS MUG**

1½ ounces brandy or bourbon

¾ ounce fresh lemon juice

¼ ounce Hunt + Alpine Cardamom-Coriander Syrup (see page 74)

½ ounce ginger syrup (see below)

3 ounces hot water

Orange twist and cinnamon stick, for garnish

Preheat a glass mug by filling it with hot water. Leave the water in for now and set it aside.

To prepare the drink, you'll want a heat-conducting vessel that fits into a second container. Two metal mixing tins work great: fill the first with enough hot water that the second container floats in the water when placed inside the first. Essentially, you are creating a small bain-marie to preheat the ingredients without diluting them.

Add the brandy or bourbon, lemon juice, cardamom-coriander syrup, and ginger syrup to your mixing tins and stir gently until heated through.

Empty the water from the preheated mug and immediately fill it with the heated cocktail. Top with 3 ounces hot water. Express the orange twist over the drink, and place the cinnamon stick and twist in the drink.

GINGER SYRUP

Ginger syrup is an easy ingredient to make and keep in your refrigerator. It adds a spicy pop of ginger to any drink. The following recipe easily surpasses most commercially-available products, which are often too sweet or devoid of the spiciness we love from ginger. Simply combine equal parts (by weight) whole ginger, white sugar, and hot water into a blender container. Cap the blender and turn on high until the mixture no longer has chunks of ginger, usually about 2 minutes. Then strain the syrup of the remaining fibers with a fine strainer or colander (do not use a coffee filter, as the sugar will make it nearly impossible for the slurry to pass through the filter). Keep the syrup bottled and chilled in the refrigerator for up to 2 weeks.

HOT BUTTERED RUM

There is something about the cold that makes people stick to what they know; hot toddy, hot buttered rum, and Irish coffee orders abound in the winter. We always try to offer the best possible version of each of these drinks.

YIELD: 1 DRINK ∽ **GLASS: GLASS MUG**

2 tablespoons Hot Buttered Rum Mix (recipe follows)

3–4 ounces hot water, divided

1½ ounces dark rum

Freshly grated nutmeg, for garnish

Preheat a glass mug by filling it with hot water. Let it sit until the cup heats through, then dump out the water.

Add the Hot Buttered Rum Mix into the preheated mug and add a small amount (about an ounce) of the hot water. Stir with a small whisk until the mix is incorporated into the water.

Add the rum and fill the mug with the remaining hot water. Stir with the whisk to fully incorporate. Garnish with freshly grated nutmeg and serve.

HOT BUTTERED RUM MIX

YIELD: 1 PINT

½ pound unsalted butter, softened to room temperature

1 cup high-quality vanilla ice cream

½ cup dark brown sugar

2 black cardamom pods, grated

1½ teaspoons freshly grated nutmeg

1½ teaspoons freshly grated cinnamon

SPECIAL EQUIPMENT: *This recipe requires an electric or stand mixer to ensure an even consistency.*

Combine the butter, ice cream, brown sugar, cardamom, nutmeg, and cinnamon in the bowl of a stand mixer with a paddle attachment. If using an electric hand mixer, combine all ingredients in a bowl.

Mix on low to medium speed until fully incorporated, about 2 minutes. If there are a few small chunks of butter, that's okay.

Use the mix immediately, or store it in an airtight container in the freezer, softening it slightly before use by setting it out at room temperature long enough to make scooping easy, about 5 minutes. This recipe will keep, frozen, for up to 3 weeks.

SPANISH COFFEE

With its roots in the Pacific Northwest, Spanish Coffee is an underappreciated American classic. This drink is just as popular for its taste as for its presentation. The team at the stalwart Portland, Oregon, restaurant and bar Huber's has mastered the art of presentation on this, with bartenders coming tableside and building the drink with a fantastic flourish.

YIELD: 1 DRINK ↝ **GLASS: GLASS MUG**

Orange slice, for the rim

Superfine sugar, for the rim

1 ounce overproof rum (151 or similar proof)

¾ ounce orange liqueur (we use Pierre Ferrand Dry Curaçao)

¾ ounce coffee liqueur (we use Allen's Coffee Flavored Brandy, see page 164)

4 ounces hot coffee

Freshly whipped cream

Ground cinnamon and nutmeg, combined equal parts in a shaker

Wet the rim of a heatproof, tall-sided glass mug with an orange slice, and roll the outside edge of the glass in superfine sugar.

Pour the overproof rum into the glass, and while holding the glass at an angle, light it on fire with a stick lighter. Immediately put the lighter down. Slowly rotate the glass in your hand to allow oxygen to feed the flame and allow the flame to gently caramelize the sugar rim.

NOTE: *The key to this drink is using the flame to caramelize the sugar on the rim of the glass without burning it. You need to act quickly and decisively in your preparation. If you tilt the glass at an angle, you can easily light the rum. Once it's lit, you want to hold the bottom of the glass (the sides will get hot!) and slowly rotate it in your hand to continually provide fresh oxygen to the flame and evenly caramelize the sugars. As the drink burns, you are slowly burning off some of the alcohol in the rum and bringing the proof down.*

Once the sugar is caramelized, gently pour the orange and coffee liqueurs into the glass. The flame should continue to burn during this step.

Top the glass with hot coffee. Garnish with the whipped cream and a shake of the cinnamon-nutmeg, and serve. If you do this correctly, the fully made drink will still have a small flame before you top it with whipped cream. (Caution to you and your guests: the rim will be predictably hot for a couple of moments.)

FIRE SAFETY FOR BARTENDERS

Since you will be lighting things on fire, it pays to practice proper safety procedures whether you're in a restaurant or at the home bar.

- Prepare for the Worst: Keep a bucket of water and a fire extinguisher nearby.

- Stay Flame Free: Make sure your hair is pulled back and loose pieces of clothing are secured.

- Get Ready: Make sure your ingredients are all within arm's reach.

- Really Get Ready: Try a dry run without fire before you try it for real.

- Keep It Clean: This is not a cocktail to make once you've had a few behind the home bar!

SUMMER IN OULU

After opening, Hunt + Alpine was named by *Imbibe* magazine to the 2014 class of Imbibe 75, the magazine's list of the people, places, and flavors they believe will shape the year. Our friends at Tandem Coffee were also included. (They have an amazing bakery that you shouldn't miss on a trip to Portland!) We wanted to create a cocktail to celebrate this recognition, and well, we think coffee cocktails are pretty rad.

YIELD: 1 DRINK ❧ **GLASS: DOUBLE OLD FASHIONED**

1½ ounces aquavit (we make our own—see page 135—but Krogstad, from Portland, Oregon, is a great buy)

¾ ounce Fernet-Branca

2 ounces cold-pressed coffee (or just cold coffee; you don't want the hot stuff)

Whipped Cream (see page 159)

Pinch of grated black cardamom, for garnish

Combine the aquavit, Fernet-Branca, and coffee in a double old fashioned glass.

Add ice and gently stir to incorporate and chill. Top with the freshly whipped cream and grated black cardamom and serve.

RICCIPURRA (RICE PUDDING)

Briana grew up across the street from her grandparents. Every Sunday, her grandmother and great-grandmother (whom she called mummu) would make this luxurious rice pudding. She would rush across the street to watch them tend to the pot, waiting for it to be ready. Every time we cook this for our children, it reminds her of all the Sundays she'd spend sitting on the kitchen table, waiting for the pudding to be ready.

We've found that you can serve this recipe multiple ways. Briana always enjoyed it served warm as a kid. However, serving it cold with fruit soup (see page 89) or with goat cheese and fruit is also delicious. This recipe is incredibly versatile.

YIELD: 8 SERVINGS, EACH 6 OUNCES

---

5 cups whole milk

1 cup medium-grain white rice

Large pinch of salt

OPTIONAL ADDITIONS

Brown sugar, about ¼ cup (or to taste)

Maple syrup, about ¼ cup (or to taste)

Goat cheese, at room temperature, about ½ cup (or to taste)

In a large pot, slowly warm the milk on low heat. Some people like to use a double boiler, but we find that if you're willing to pay close attention, you don't need one. Once the milk is warm but not boiling, add the rice and salt.

Let the milk and rice cook slowly, stirring occasionally, being careful to not let it burn and never letting the milk get to a full boil. Once the rice has absorbed all the milk and the texture is creamy and smooth, you can remove the mixture from the heat. This should take about an hour and a half.

If you're making a sweet dessert riccipurra, you can immediately add brown sugar or maple syrup to the pot, stirring until it is well blended. These ingredients are added to taste, so we recommend starting with about ¼ cup and then adding more if needed. If you are making this savory, add the room-temperature goat cheese, starting with about ½ cup, and mix well.

Serve immediately, while still warm. If you'd prefer to serve cold, spoon the pudding into individual bowls and refrigerate, covered, for 3 hours to overnight. See the finished product on the next page.

FINNISH FRUIT SOUP

It might seem a little crazy to use dried fruit to make this recipe, especially when we have such easy access to fresh fruit and berries almost year round. Yet dried fruit really does make the best base for this unique "soup." You can serve it cold on its own, but we prefer it warmed up atop a bowl of fresh Riccipurra (see page 87).

YIELD: 8 SERVINGS (AS A TOPPING TO RICCIPURRA)

3 cups mixed dried fruit (we like to use dried apples, raisins, and apricots, though prunes are a traditional ingredient as well)

1–2 cinnamon sticks (depending on the size and strength of the sticks)

1 teaspoon freshly ground cardamom

½ teaspoon nutmeg

½ cup sugar, or more to taste

Pinch of freshly ground black pepper

1½ tablespoons potato starch

Apple cider vinegar, to taste

Soak the dried fruit overnight in a large bowl with 6 cups water. The fruit will absorb the water and become much larger. If any pieces become larger than bite size, remove them from the water and cut them into smaller pieces.

Pour the fruit and water into a large pot. Add the cinnamon sticks, cardamom, nutmeg, and sugar, along with a pinch of freshly ground black pepper. Cook over medium-high heat until the mixture comes to a boil, and stir until the sugar is dissolved. There should be enough liquid in the pot to cover the fruit. If you need to add more water, do so now. Reduce the heat to low so the mixture is at a simmer.

Mix the potato starch with a little water to create a slurry, then add it to the soup, stirring well to incorporate. Keep simmering until the liquid thickens. Once the liquid thickens to a syrupy consistency and the fruit aroma is strong, add the apple cider vinegar to taste. We typically add 1 to 2 teaspoons.

Serve the soup warm, or chill it, covered, in the refrigerator and serve once it's cool.

SWEDISH MEATBALLS

Swedish meatballs are a classic that almost everyone has enjoyed at some point. We prepare ours a using a blend of meats and spices and serve them over homemade spaetzle. It's a hearty dish that can work as a filling appetizer or as a main dish and has been incredibly popular since making its debut on the Hunt + Alpine menu. This is a crowd pleaser that will stick to your ribs.

YIELD: 4 SERVINGS (ABOUT 12 MEATBALLS)

MEATBALLS

2 cups panko

¼ cup milk

½ pound ground pork

1 pound ground veal, beef, or venison, or a mixture

2 egg yolks

¼ cup grated Parmesan cheese

¼ teaspoon ground nutmeg

1 teaspoon black pepper

1½ tablespoons salt

Preheat your oven to 350°F, and line a large rimmed baking sheet with parchment paper. Set the baking sheet aside.

Add the panko and milk to a small mixing bowl. Mix briefly and allow to sit for a minute. You want the milk to hydrate the panko until it's porridge-like.

Combine the pork, veal, eggs, and panko mixture in a large bowl or in the bowl of a stand mixer. Mix by hand or with the paddle attachment on low speed until fully incorporated. Add the cheese, nutmeg, pepper, and salt.

Turn the mixer off and scrape down the sides with a spatula. Run the mixer on medium speed for 1 minute, or combine by hand.

Use a spoon to scoop the meatball mixture and form each meatball gently by hand. (We like large tablespoon-size meatballs.) Space the meatballs 1 inch apart on the prepared baking sheet.

Bake for 15 minutes for tablespoon-size meatballs. (It may take longer if you make larger meatballs.) They should read 165° with an instant-read thermometer.

SPAETZLE

3 cups bread flour

1 cup rye flour

1 cup milk

8 eggs

½ teaspoon nutmeg

Pinch of salt

Pinch of freshly ground black pepper

Combine the bread flour, rye flour, milk, eggs, and a pinch each of salt and pepper in the bowl of a stand mixer. Using the paddle attachment, mix for 5 minutes on low speed. If mixing by hand, combine all ingredients into a large bowl and stir until evenly mixed.

While the mixer is running, put a large pot of lightly salted water over medium-high heat and bring to a boil.

Stop the mixer after 5 minutes and wait for the water to come to a boil. Prepare an ice bath for the finished spaetzle and set it aside. Once the water is boiling, working in small batches, push the spaetzle dough through a perforated pan into the pot of boiling water. You can use a dough scraper to help push the dough through. Work in batches so as not to overfill your boiling water. You should aim to create 1 layer of spaetzle per batch.

Cook about 4 minutes, until spaetzle floats to the surface. Immediately remove the spaetzle with a slotted spoon or strainer and transfer to an ice bath. Repeat with the remaining spaetzle dough. When finished, strain any excess water and toss with a neutral oil before serving.

DEMI-GLACE

5 pounds beef marrow bones

2 cups dry red wine

1 tablespoon neutral oil

2 large onions, chopped

2 large carrots, chopped

1 bunch fresh thyme (or a pinch of dried thyme)

Preheat the oven to 350°F. Roast the marrow bones on a large rimmed baking sheet until dark brown, about 20 minutes.

Meanwhile, heat the oil in a large pot (the marrow bones will need to fit after they've roasted) over low heat until shimmering, add the onions and carrots, and cook until they start to caramelize, about 15 minutes.

Once the onions are golden brown, add the red wine and continue to cook. Increase heat to medium and cook the liquid until it is thick, fragrant, and reduced by more than half, approximately 10 minutes.

By now, the marrow bones should have finished roasting. Add them to the sauce along with any liquid that has roasted off and enough water to cover the bones. Bring the sauce to a simmer and skim the foam and impurities from the surface from time to time, simmering for approximately 15 minutes.

When the broth is thoroughly skimmed and at a simmer, add the thyme. Turn up the heat and bring to a boil.

Cook until the broth has thickened, approximately 20 minutes. Using a strainer set over a large bowl, strain the broth and discard the bones. Return the strained liquid to the pot and reduce by half. Remove from the heat and set aside until the rest of the Swedish Meatball Sauce (recipe follows) is ready for it.

SWEDISH MEATBALL SAUCE

4 tablespoons butter

1 large onion, finely diced

¼ cup Demi-Glace (recipe above)

1 quart heavy cream

Salt, to taste, approximately 1 teaspoon

Freshly ground black pepper, to taste, approximately 1 teaspoon

Pinch of freshly grated nutmeg, approximately ¼ teaspoon

In a large pot, melt the butter over low heat and add the diced onion. Sweat the onion until it turns translucent, about 12 minutes.

Increase the heat to medium high. Add the demi-glace and cream. Bring the mixture to a simmer.

Season with salt, fresh cracked pepper, and nutmeg.

MEATBALL SOUP

A twist on both Swedish Meatballs and Italian Wedding Soup, our Meatball Soup recipe can be cooked ahead of time so it's ready when you and your guests come in from the cold. The broth is earthy and comforting, and it takes the meatballs in a different direction than the sauce on page 93. We love making this for friends because it's simple to cook yet impressive and filling.

YIELD: 4 SERVINGS

1 cup pearled barley

1½ teaspoons salt, to taste

2 tablespoons neutral oil, such as canola

1 large onion, diced

1 head garlic, with top removed to expose cloves

4 dried shiitake mushrooms

5 pounds beef bones

1 recipe Swedish Meatballs (see page 91)

Combine the barley, salt, and 2½ cups water in a small pot. Bring to boil over medium-high heat, and then reduce to a simmer. Simmer the barley until the water has been absorbed into the barley or evaporated, about 35 minutes. Spread the barley into a thin layer on a rimmed baking sheet to cool.

Meanwhile, while the barley cooks and cools, heat a large stockpot over medium heat, add oil until shimmering, add onions, and immediately reduce heat to low. Cook, stirring occasionally, until caramelized, about 25 minutes.

Add to the onions 5 quarts water, the garlic, the dried shiitakes, and the beef bones. Increase the heat to medium high and simmer until the broth has reduced by about 1 quart, approximately 10 minutes. Skim any foam or impurities from the top of the broth from time to time.

After the broth has reduced, remove the bones and discard. Add the meatballs and barley to the broth, simmering for at least 10 minutes before serving. The soup can then be served immediately, or you can take it off the heat, refrigerate, and reheat to serve the next day.

APRÈS SKI (OR GETTING COZY)

Ski culture in Maine is just as big a part of life as the ocean or Allen's Coffee Flavored Brandy. So it makes sense that *après ski*, the culture of ending the day with the people you've spent all day out in the cold with, is something we partake in whether we've skied or not. Grabbing a drink and something to eat with friends after a day spent outdoors is a ritual for many.

When you step into Hunt + Alpine, you'll find two very large handcrafted dark wood tables. These were made to evoke that feeling of comfort and create a sense of community inside the bar. Getting toasty, in every sense, with a drink is the first step. And the same goes for our food. It's no coincidence we serve dishes named Skier or Hunter that are shareable feasts for a group. We want to bring you together with shared experiences over food and drinks.

When après skiing at home, it's important to get a hearty meal out quickly. In these situations, we recommend preparing a large, one-pot meal or getting the group together to cook over an open fire. The fire crackling while everyone stands around cooking their own sausage is peak comfort after a chilly day.

CHAPTER 5

THE COFFEE TABLE

We love variety. That's why when you visit us at Hunt + Alpine (or our home), you'll see drinks that range from the classic Old Fashioned to originals such as the Fratelli Stinger. We feel the same way about the food we serve too. One of our favorite ways to show off this variety and let our guests experience a wide breadth of choice is by recreating our version of the Finnish coffee table with a modern, Maine version of the classic smorgasbord. With so much variety and so many different flavors, you are bound to make even picky eaters happy.

Every time Briana's mother, Bee, talks about her trips to visit relatives in Finland, she will, without fail, mention the open-faced sandwiches served on thick slices of rye bread with pickles and cold cuts. She loved them. She'll also mention how she could eat them for breakfast, lunch, and dinner. When we were creating the food menu for Hunt + Alpine, Bee's story of the coffee table spread, also known as a smorgasbord, came to mind.

THE BIGGER THE BETTER

There is no wrong way to put a smorgasbord together, but there is such a thing as making it too small. When we are building ours, we do so on very large, thick wooden boards. The completed spread should look like something that could feed a table of Vikings (or Mainers) after a long day out in the elements. Always go big, with an abundance of each item. Here are a few other observations:

- You can never have too many pickles to go with your rye bread and crackers.

- We've found that Gravlax (page 109) is often the first thing to disappear.

- Be aware that some people like a lot of condiments when they build open-faced sandwiches.

- Salads are a wonderful way to add greens that aren't pickled.

Last but certainly not least, include a surprise. We like to bring shots of aquavit to the table, and we always include steamed clams when they are in season. Adding a warm dish or two brings the smorgasbord out of the snack realm and makes it feel like a well-rounded meal.

FRATELLI STINGER

One of our earliest Hunt + Alpine originals, this is our riff on the classic Stinger. While the Stinger is generally double strained, we choose to strain ours just once because we love the texture of the ice crystals in it. It's also one of the few Hunt + Alpine drinks that goes against the rules of stirring versus straining (see page 6), which keeps it in line with the classic Stinger cocktail. Despite being only spirits and other stirrable ingredients, this drink is shaken due to the thickness of the syrup (in the original, this would be the crème de menthe). If you like rules and structure, as we do, it's easiest to think of the crème de menthe in the original Stinger recipe as a nondairy dairy ingredient; therefore, you need to shake instead of stir this drink. We decided to honor the original Stinger recipe by shaking this drink and preserving the layer of ice chips that frost the top of the drink. Additionally, shaking this drink aerates the ingredients and helps it go down quickly. It's a great drink to open the palate and get your appetite going . . . and going, and going.

YIELD: 1 DRINK ✺ **GLASS: CHILLED COCKTAIL**

2 ounces applejack

¾ ounce Branca Menta

½ ounce bonded bourbon

1 teaspoon rich simple syrup (see page 191)

1 dash Angostura bitters

Lemon peel, for garnish

Combine the applejack, Branca Menta, bourbon, syrup, and bitters in a mixing tin.

Fill the tin with ice, cap, and shake hard for 20 seconds.

Strain the drink into a chilled cocktail glass, garnish with an expressed lemon peel, and serve.

HUNT + ALPINE
GIBSON

There's very little in the way of tricks to this drink; we're using a classic formulation and simply tweaking the ingredients slightly. What is important, as with all classics and three-ingredient drinks, is to be very precise about your measurements and use fresh, quality ingredients. Here we've chosen to use Old Tom gin instead of the classic London dry. Old Tom is a style that predates the classic London dry; it's the missing link between genever, a Dutch product distilled from malt and juniper in the mash, and London dry, a product made from a neutral grain spirit with juniper and other flavors added after distillation. Old Tom–style gin tends to be slightly sweeter than London dry, with a more restrained juniper note. Occasionally Old Tom gin is aged in barrels, but when it's unaged, as we use below, it offers a clean, bright palette on which to paint a crisp cocktail.

Just as important as the choice of gin in this drink is the choice of vermouth. In our house Gibson recipe, we use Noilly Prat, a classic dry vermouth with a strong herbal backbone. We feel this balances out the softness in the Old Tom gin and ties the drink well to the cocktail onions. Additionally, we use a dash of orange bitters and express an orange peel over the drink to highlight the citrus found in both the gin and the vermouth.

YIELD: 1 DRINK ⌁ GLASS: CHILLED ROCKS GLASS

2 ounces Old Tom–style gin (we prefer Tanqueray)

¾ ounce dry vermouth (we prefer a robust, classically dry vermouth such as Noilly Prat)

1 dash orange bitters (we use Regan's No. 6)

Orange peel and Cocktail Onions (recipe follows), for garnish

Combine the gin, vermouth, and bitters in a chilled 10-ounce rocks glass.

Add a large ice cube or several small cubes and stir 30 to 40 times.

Express the orange peel over the drink, skewer both the peel and a cocktail onion or two on a cocktail pick, garnish, and serve.

COCKTAIL ONIONS

1 dozen pearl onions (pick the smallest onions you can find)

2 cups distilled white vinegar

1 tablespoon kosher salt

2 tablespoons juniper berries

1 tablespoon fennel seeds

1 orange, halved

Peel the pearl onions and place them in a heatproof container, such as a small glass mixing bowl or large glass measuring cup.

Combine the vinegar, 1 cup water, and salt in a small pot and bring to a boil over medium-high heat. Meanwhile, toast the juniper berries and fennel seeds on a small rimmed baking sheet under an oven broiler until aromatic. It should take only a minute or two.

Once the pickling liquid is boiling, add the juniper and fennel. Squeeze the juice from the orange halves into the pot as well, and then drop the spent orange halves into the pot.

Turn off the heat and carefully pour the liquid, orange halves, and herbs over the onions. Allow the onions to rest for at least 30 minutes, or up 2 hours, at room temperature. Transfer the mixture to an airtight container and store in the refrigerator for up to 1 month. For ease of serving, it can be helpful to strain off the herbs and orange halves.

ON VERMOUTH

Vermouth should be treated like a bottle of wine. It is not shelf stable and certainly should not be stored open at room temperature for any length of time. If you don't anticipate using much vermouth at your house, buy a smaller bottle; most good vermouths are sold in 375ml bottles, which will make you about a dozen martinis, Manhattans, or Gibsons, depending on your preference. If you find yourself with a bottle reaching a week or two after opening, pour yourself a glass of it over ice with a splash of soda water and a wedge of fruit (orange or grapefruit work nicely) and enjoy it while cooking your next dinner.

GRAVLAX

This is one of the most traditional recipes we serve at Hunt + Alpine. Our gravlax has strong notes of caraway and dill, which means it goes great with heavier breads and aquavit. It's simple to make, but it does take two to three days to cure. Just remember to plan ahead—it's worth it.

YIELD: APPROXIMATELY 8 APPETIZER-SIZED SERVINGS

1 side of salmon (skin on), about 1 pound

4 cups kosher salt

2 cups sugar

¼ cup ground black pepper

1 tablespoon toasted caraway seeds

1 tablespoon dill seed

1 teaspoon celery seed

½ tablespoon red pepper flakes

1 bunch fresh dill, chopped, approximately ¼ cup

Remove all pin bones from the salmon and discard them. Thoroughly combine the salt, sugar, pepper, caraway seeds, dill seed, celery seed, red pepper flakes, and chopped dill in a large mixing bowl, then divide and sprinkle half of the cure mixture on the bottom of a rectangular nonreactive container with a cover.

Place the salmon on top of the cure with the skin side down. Cover the salmon with the remaining cure mix. Place a heavy weight, such as a plate, on top of the salmon, refrigerate, and let cure for 48 to 72 hours.

When fully cured, the salmon should be very firm to the touch. Remove it from the cure mixture and wash off the salt and spices. Dry thoroughly with clean linen or paper towels. Wrap the salmon in cheesecloth and store it in the refrigerator until you're ready to serve. This keeps for a month under refrigeration. We suggest slicing some and serving it with crackers, cream cheese, and dill—or on an open-faced sandwich.

PAIRING COCKTAILS WITH FOOD

When you have so many choices on a smorgasbord, it's easy to fall into the trap of not thinking too hard about the drinks. However, you'll need cocktails that will stand up to strong flavors (such as pickles) without overpowering them, and the drinks should help whet the appetite. In our opinion, this should be the case any time you're drinking with a meal—pairings are important. Just like a sommelier pairs wine with a meal, we love to thoughtfully pair cocktails.

Pairing drinks with your meal doesn't have to be complicated, but it should be well thought out. With wine, if you stick to a few basic rules, pairing can be a cinch. Cocktails are the same in that sense, and we feel pairing drinks with food should be fun rather than fussy. Here are a few basic ideas to use as a guide.

THINK ABOUT THE WEIGHT OF FLAVORS. Whether you think about it or not, everything you consume has a weight on the palate. Some food and drink is lighter, some heavier. A crisp martini and seared trout fall into a very different category than an Old Fashioned and grilled steak. When pairing cocktails with food, be aware of the heaviness of the flavors, and try to keep drink and food in the same realm. It very rarely works to pair a heavy cocktail with a light food or vice versa.

PICK FLAVORS TO HIGHLIGHT. Instead of trying to make an exact match with a dish and a cocktail, think about a specific flavor that defines either the food or the drink for you. Pick that flavor and use it as a thread to tie the pairing together. For instance, if you're making Cucumber Salad (page 123), you may pick up strongly on the fennel seeds that are tossed with the onions and want to highlight that flavor. An easy way to get the essence of fennel or anise in a drink is through a spritz or rinse of absinthe, which can be found in numerous drinks in this book, from the 1840 Sazerac (see page 16) to the Late Night at OOB #1 or #2 (see page 177).

DON'T BE AFRAID OF ACIDITY, BITTERNESS, OR ALCOHOL. When it comes to food and drink pairings, we often talk about varying levels of acidity, bitterness, and alcohol. It can seem counterintuitive to use such strong flavors, but they can be leveraged to pair with food that is fatty or rich. Rich and fatty foods eaten on their own can coat your palate and cover up some of the flavors of a dish, but acidity, bitterness, or simply high-proof spirits can cut through that richness and allow you to enjoy both drink and food further. One of our favorite Hunt + Alpine pairings is pouring a Norseman (see page 131) alongside a pile of gravlax (see page 109).

CONSIDER THE COMPLEXITY OF FLAVORS. Some thought should be put into how complex a dish or drink is, and you should be wary of pairing two multilayered items together. Complex flavors in cocktails and food often mean complex or time-consuming preparations. That's nothing that we shy away from, yet it can be a waste of time and energy if you make a stunning dish and put it together with an equally stunning cocktail. Chances are the subtlety and complexity of one or the other will be lost because both are so complex. Instead, if you have a drink that has multiple layers that you're proud of and want to highlight, pair it with a simpler dish.

DON'T GET WASTED. We always discuss with our new staff the responsibility that comes with serving others alcohol. It can be very easy to get caught up in the fun of discovering new drink flavors and combinations and forget that what we're serving and consuming can really hurt the next day. Be kind to your guests' livers and make sure to moderate their intake. This can take many forms: half-poured cocktails at each course instead of a full three-ounce drink, low-proof drinks spritzed throughout the pairings, or beer or wine with a mid-course dish instead of a cocktail. Note that this doesn't have to mean you have less fun. One of our favorite cocktail pairing experiences was when we had the honor to celebrate Repeal Day at the James Beard House in New York City. Hunt + Alpine was the first cocktail bar asked to cook the entire meal for guests, along with making and serving drink pairings. We served many of our favorite cocktails, but about halfway through the meal, we brought out lobster bibs for everyone and served steamed clams alongside a can of one of our favorite beers (Bunker Brewing's Machine). Everyone appreciated the levity and taste of Maine, and I'm sure the guests were thrilled to have a reprieve from cocktails for a moment as well.

BE WHIMSICAL. Our final words of advice on cocktail and food pairings is that they truly should be fun, not something to stress over. Sometimes a pairing doesn't work out exactly as you may have hoped, but if you have good food and good drink, it shouldn't get in the way of a good time.

PICKLE RECIPES

We love pickles! From Bread and Butters to Cider Pickles to Dilly Beans, pickles are a great accompaniment to most dishes we serve. They are also great drinking food. What follows are some of our favorite pickle recipes that we have developed over the years.

Use these recipes as written or as a starting point to pickle whatever fruits or vegetables you have in abundance. Note that we've stuck to producing and providing recipes for quick pickles, which all follow the same basic process below. Simply follow these directions for all of the recipes except for the kimchi.

YIELD: APPROXIMATELY 2 CUPS OF PICKLES PER RECIPE

QUICK PICKLE HOW-TO

1. Place all liquid ingredients in a medium-size pot. Bring the mixture to a boil over medium heat.

2. While the liquid is coming to a boil, clean, trim, and slice your vegetables (or fruit) to your preferred thickness and shape. We typically use a mandoline for thinner cuts and a knife and cutting board for thicker ones. We've provided suggestions for each type of pickle on the pages that follow. Place them in a clean, heatproof container that's large enough to hold all of your liquid. Set aside.

3. Add all dry ingredients, including any herbs, to the simmering pot. Stir until the sugar and salt have dissolved. Reduce the heat and keep at a bare simmer for 10 minutes to infuse.

4. Pour the hot liquid, with herbs, over your cleaned, sliced produce and allow to stand at room temperature for 20 minutes.

   NOTE: *Depending on your serving preference, you can strain the liquid of the herbs during this step.*

5. Once the mixture cools, cover and transfer to the refrigerator. Your pickles will keep in the fridge for at least 1 month, but you'll be tempted to finish them sooner.

CUCUMBER PICKLES

Everyone thinks of dill first, but there is an amazing variety of pickles using cucumbers. The Cider Pickles in particular are always on hand at our house for snacking. Read on for the recipe and a few of our other favorites.

CIDER PICKLES

2 European cucumbers, cleaned and sliced into thin rounds (we go to about ¼ inch on a mandoline, though you can get just as thin with a sharp kitchen knife)

2 tablespoons kosher salt

2 cups good-quality apple cider vinegar (we use Bragg's)

1 cup water

SWEET PICKLES

2 European cucumbers, cleaned and sliced into rounds (about ½ inch thick)

2 cups white vinegar

1 cup water

1 cup sugar

2 tablespoons kosher salt

BREAD AND BUTTER PICKLES

2 European cucumbers, cleaned and sliced into rounds (about ½ inch thick; we use a crinkle-edged knife for these)

2 cups apple cider vinegar

½ cup distilled white vinegar or rice wine vinegar

1 cup water

1 cup sugar

¼ cup kosher salt

2 teaspoons celery seed

2 teaspoons ground turmeric

2 teaspoons pickling spice

1 teaspoon mustard seeds

½ teaspoon red pepper flakes

SAVORY PICKLES

2 European cucumbers, cleaned and sliced into rounds (about ½ inch thick)

2 cups distilled white vinegar

1 cup water

2 tablespoons kosher salt

1 teaspoon red pepper flakes

1 tablespoon mustard seeds

DILL PICKLES

2 European cucumbers, cleaned and sliced into thin rounds (we go to about ¼ inch on a mandoline, though you can get just as thin with a sharp kitchen knife)

2 cups distilled white vinegar

¾ cup water

2 tablespoons kosher salt

1 teaspoon red pepper flakes

1 tablespoon mustard seeds

1 bunch fresh dill

1 tablespoon dill seed

3 cloves garlic

OTHER VEGETABLES

We all know pickles shouldn't end with cucumbers, right? What follows are a few of our favorites, including Dilly Beans, Pickled Fennel, and even a quick kimchi.

DILLY BEANS

2 cups cleaned and trimmed green beans

2 cups distilled white vinegar

1 cup water

2 tablespoons kosher salt

1 teaspoon red pepper flakes

1 tablespoon mustard seeds

½ bunch fresh dill

1 tablespoon dill seed

3 cloves garlic

PICKLED SHALLOTS

2 cups peeled, trimmed, and thinly sliced shallots (about ¼ inch thick)

2 cups distilled white vinegar

1 cup water

½ cup sugar

2 tablespoons kosher salt

PICKLED FENNEL

2 cups sliced fennel, with fronds and core removed (about ¼ inch thick)

2 cups sherry vinegar

1 cup water

½ cup sugar

2 tablespoons kosher salt

1 tablespoon dry vermouth (optional)

Peel of ½ an orange (optional)

PICKLED RED ONIONS

2 cups peeled, trimmed, and thinly sliced red onions (about ¼ inch thick)

1 cup red wine vinegar

1 cup water

½ cup sugar

2 tablespoons kosher salt

3 limes, halved (squeeze them by hand into the pot and leave the spent halves to steep with the onions for 20 minutes before removing)

FRUIT AND OTHER TYPES

There is something really fun about pickled fruit. It's great as a garnish for cocktails, as part of salads, or even eaten plain. The sweetness and touch of sour complement each other nicely. We've always enjoyed the unexpected treat of pickling fruit whenever we find ourselves with a bounty from the farm.

PICKLED GREEN STRAWBERRIES

1 quart green strawberries, cleaned, hulled, and cut lengthwise

1 cup apple cider vinegar

1 cup distilled white vinegar

¼ cup honey

2 tablespoons kosher salt

1 cup water

16 bay leaves

8 teaspoons black peppercorns

8 teaspoons yellow mustard seeds

4 teaspoons caraway seeds

CUCUMBER AND APPLE KIMCHI

❗ **NOTE:** *This recipe has different instructions than the rest of the pickles—see below.*

2 European cucumbers, cleaned and peeled

1 tablespoon sugar

1 teaspoon kosher salt

1 tablespoon Aleppo or Korean chili powder

1 knob ginger (about 1 inch), peeled and diced

1 apple, peeled, cored, and chopped to ½-inch pieces

1 tablespoon minced garlic

¼ cup fish sauce

1 teaspoon sriracha

Halve the cucumbers, scrape out the seeds, and slice them into ½-inch slices. Toss the cucumbers with the sugar and salt and place in a colander over the sink or a bowl to allow the water to drain from the vegetables.

Quickly blend in a blender or mash to a paste with a mortar and pestle (or in a bowl with the back of a fork) the chili powder, ginger, apple, garlic, fish sauce, and sriracha to a paste.

After 30 minutes of draining the salted cucumbers, transfer them to a bowl and toss the cucumbers with the paste. Cover and allow to sit in the refrigerator for 3 days.

This will keep in the fridge for up to 1 month.

RYE CRACKERS

Some restaurants are known for their bread; we have always preferred to serve this cracker instead. It's a lighter, modern version of crispbread, a heavy rye cracker traditional in Finland and Sweden. We love this version because it holds up next to even the strongest cocktails and pickles—perfect for our menu.

YIELD: ABOUT 2 DOZEN CRACKERS

2 cups warm water

1 package (0.25 ounce) instant yeast

2 cups rye flour

2 cups all-purpose flour

2 tablespoons sea salt, divided

1 tablespoon nigella (black sesame) seeds

1 tablespoon sesame seeds

1 tablespoon caraway seeds

2 tablespoons extra-virgin olive oil

SPECIAL EQUIPMENT: *This recipe requires a stand mixer. Ideally you'll also use a pasta machine or pasta attachment on your stand mixer, though it can be done with patience and a rolling pin.*

Combine the water and yeast in the bowl of a stand mixer and let the yeast hydrate for 5 minutes.

With the paddle attachment and the mixer running on medium speed, add the rye flour, all-purpose flour, and 1 tablespoon sea salt. Mix for about 4 minutes, or until thoroughly combined. Stop the mixer and let the dough rest, covered, for 30 minutes.

Preheat the oven to 350°F. Grease several large baking sheets well, and set aside.

Remove the dough from the bowl, and transfer it to a floured surface on your counter. Cut it into small, palm-size portions and flatten them out on the counter. Working with one piece at a time, roll each piece through a pasta machine, going from pasta attachment #1 through #2, #3, #4, and #5, to a thickness of approximately 1/16 inch. Alternatively, use a rolling pin on a floured surface to achieve a similar thickness. Cut the dough down to a few inches wide by 6 inches long.

Combine the remaining sea salt, nigella seeds, sesame seeds, and caraway seeds in a small bowl.

Transfer the dough pieces to the prepared baking sheets. Brush the oil on top of the crackers and sprinkle generously with the seed and salt mixture.

Press the seeds gently into the dough, and bake at for about 15 minutes, rotating the pans halfway through. The crackers are done when the edges are browned and they are crispy all the way through. Remove from the oven and transfer to a cooling rack. Keep in an airtight container for up to 4 days at room temperature.

HOMEMADE PRETZELS

We think these pretzels are the best we've ever had. They are soft and especially great right out of the oven. We're traditionalists and serve them with brown mustard, but they can handle anything you put on them. Don't let this recipe fool you. It might seem complicated to make pretzels, but it really isn't, and using lye isn't as scary as you might think.

YIELD: ABOUT 12 PRETZELS

1 package (0.25 ounce) active dry yeast

¼ cup sugar

2 cups IPA (or other hoppy beer)

2 cups warm water

8 cups all-purpose flour, divided

1 tablespoon kosher salt

2 eggs

1 egg white

½ cup (2 sticks) unsalted butter, at room temperature

1 ounce food-grade lye

1 tablespoon coarse (pretzel) salt

Combine the yeast, sugar, IPA, and warm water in a large glass mixing bowl. Let sit for 5 minutes to hydrate the yeast.

Add 4 cups flour and mix well. Cover the bowl with plastic wrap. Allow the dough to rise at room temperature for approximately 1 hour.

After the rise, transfer the dough to the bowl of your stand mixer. Mix on low speed with the dough hook. Slowly add the remaining 4 cups flour and the kosher salt. When the dough starts to come together, add the whole eggs and egg white, one at a time.

Once the eggs are incorporated, add the butter in 1-inch pieces. Let the dough mix until it is smooth and elastic, about 8 minutes. You should be able to stretch it until it is translucent. If it tears, continue mixing.

When the dough is properly mixed, stop the mixer, cover the bowl with plastic wrap, and let rise for 30 minutes.

Portion the dough into 12 equal-size balls and let rest one more time on a floured countertop, covered, for 15 minutes.

Roll the dough into ½-inch-thick strands and form each piece of dough into a pretzel shape of your choosing. (We prefer the traditional clover-leaf design, which is made by braiding the 2 loose ends together twice to form a circle and laying the braid over the circle.) Freeze for at least 30 minutes on a waxed-paper-coated baking sheet. Do not skip the freezing, as it helps develop the crust.

When you're ready to bake your pretzels, let the dough come to room temperature for 10 minutes (it does not need to be fully thawed). Preheat the oven to 450°F.

Meanwhile, prepare the lye solution. Use caution when handling lye, as in strong concentration or exposure it can burn the skin. We use non-reactive containers and tongs. Pour 4 cups of water into a nonreactive container (don't use plastic here) and add the lye to the water. Submerge each pretzel in the lye solution for 5 seconds. Use metal tongs to handle the pretzels to keep the lye off of your hands. Place the prepared pretzels on a parchment-lined baking sheet.

Bake for 12 to 15 minutes, or until golden brown. Remove from the oven, brush with water, and sprinkle with coarse salt. Serve immediately. These are best the day they are baked, but can be kept covered and warmed in a 300°F oven the next day. If saving, do not garnish with salt until you are ready to serve them.

OUR FAVORITE SANDWICHES HAVE OPEN FACES

We think sandwiches are easily one of the best foods out there. We love how creative you can get with ingredients that go between two pieces of bread. The same goes for open-faced sandwiches, of course, which are what you'll find on our smorgasbord. It's funny how a sandwich just tastes better when you pile toppings as high as they'll go and throw out that top slice. (Though you are free to use a top slice too—we won't tell.)

When we design a board that's made for sandwich building, bread isn't the required carb. From bagels to rye bread to toast to pretzels and crackers, how you want to create a spread is totally up to you. Just a couple of options besides bread, or even different types of bread, can make a totally different sandwich.

If you're feeling uninspired as to what to put on your open-faced sandwich, here are a few of our favorite combinations.

Rye Bread + Smoked Trout + Dill + Pickles + Mustard

Bagels + Deviled Eggs (mash or chop them) + Bread and Butter Pickles + Pepper

Rye Crackers + Gravlax + Cream Cheese + Dill + Pepper

Rye Toast + Pork Liver Mousse + Mustard + Capers + Greens + Pickles

Pretzels (sliced horizontally in half) + Soft Cheese + Pickles (heat up the sandwich, then add pickles for something really special)

Bagels + Butter + Ham + Cheese

Rye Bread + Pickles + Pickles + More Pickles + Mustard

Toast + Meatballs + Gravy + Cocktail Onions

Crackers + Crab + Lemon + Dill

Rye Bread + Butter + Cucumber + Pepper

CUCUMBER SALAD

This recipe is all about simplicity; it showcases what a few well-chosen flavors can do. This salad makes a wonderful side to all kinds of dishes beyond the coffee table. We especially love it with meats such as steak, but this salad really helps brighten any meal that might feel heavy.

YIELD: 4 SERVINGS AS A SIDE

3 English cucumbers, sliced thin (about ¼ inch thick)

1 tablespoon kosher salt

½ cup crème fraîche

1 teaspoon ground white pepper

1 teaspoon fennel seeds

1 teaspoon anise seed

1 tablespoon finely chopped fresh dill

1 tablespoon finely chopped fresh parsley

½ cup Pickled Red Onions (see page 114), chopped

Toss the cucumbers with the salt and allow to stand in a colander in the sink (or on paper towels) for 1 to 2 hours at room temperature.

Combine the crème fraîche, white pepper, fennel, anise, dill, and parsley in a medium-size bowl and stir until evenly mixed. Pat the cucumbers dry, and then add them to the bowl along with the chopped pickled onion. Toss to combine.

Serve immediately or refrigerate. This keeps in the refrigerator, covered, for up to 3 days. Simply stir again to combine before serving.

PORK LIVER MOUSSE

Rich, decadent, and always a crowd favorite, Pork Liver Mousse is one of those classic dishes that never go out of style. Surprisingly simple to make, it will be one of the first things to disappear from your coffee table spread. This mousse adds a luxurious element to any table and can be consumed by the spoonful, on crackers, or spread on toast with pickles on top.

YIELD: 1 (6-INCH) LOAF PAN, ENOUGH FOR 10-12 APPETIZER PORTIONS

1½ pounds pork liver

½ pound bacon, cooked, with rendered fat reserved

6 eggs

1½ cups heavy cream

2 tablespoons brandy

1 tablespoon kosher salt

Preheat the oven to 300°F.

Combine the pork liver, bacon, rendered bacon fat, eggs, cream, brandy, and salt in a blender or food processor and purée until smooth, approximately 5 minutes.

Transfer the mixture to a 6-inch loaf pan. Remove any trapped air bubbles by vigorously tapping the pan on a sturdy countertop.

Cover the pan in plastic wrap and then a layer of aluminum foil. Create a steam bath by placing the loaf pan in a larger baking dish and filling the larger dish with water to 1 inch short of the rim. Place the pan in the oven and cook for 30 minutes or until the mousse is firm. If it still jiggles in the middle, it is not done and needs to cook longer.

When cooked through, remove from the oven and allow to cool. This can be kept in the pan it was cooked in, covered and in the refrigerator, for 3 days.

CHAPTER 6

AQUAVIT

If you have spent any time drinking with someone from a northern European country or traveled there as an adult, you have probably been subjected to the line of questioning that starts with "Have you ever heard of aquavit?" This soon turns into "Really?! Never heard of it?! You have GOT to try aquavit!" In turn, this leads to "Do you know why we can't find aquavit anywhere in your country? Everyone loves this stuff, if only they could try it."

Until very recently, aquavit was an elusive spirit smuggled back from Europe in backpacks and trunks. Chilled shots were poured for close friends around the table, but only small drams so that there was plenty in the bottle for next time. Thanks to Maine's restrictive liquor laws, when we opened Hunt + Alpine Club in September 2013, there was no aquavit available, so we resorted to creating our own infusion of spices to be able to serve our guests something distinctly Scandinavian (see page 135 for the recipe).

Thankfully, having pestered producers and importers over the years, we're happy to now offer several aquavit options on our backbar. In fact, thanks to the cultural shift that has occurred around spirits and cocktails, aquavit is having a bit of a moment in the States. European brands are now being professionally imported, and some quality American-made products are increasingly available as well (our friends at House Spirits in Portland, Oregon, have been making their Danish-style Krogstad for nearly a decade now).

WHAT IS AQUAVIT?

Even those who have tried aquavit have difficulty explaining exactly what it is or what it tastes like. Additionally, every northern European country has birthed various methods and styles of aquavit, making generalizing a definition more difficult. We find it easiest to start at the textbook definition and expand from there: aquavit is a spirit category that is defined by a predominant caraway flavor. From there, every producer has their own recipes and flavor additions that define them. The Danish Aalborg has a strong backbone of caraway, while the Icelandic Brennivín is much more subtle and restrained. Some producers choose to lace their aquavit with fennel and anise flavors, while others prefer more mild dill or citrus notes. Additionally, some aquavits are traditionally aged, as in the case of the Norwegian Linie, while others have special versions that see some barrel-aging, such as the wonderful Brennivín Winter Wheat from Iceland. Still, most aquavits are unaged and clear. Regardless of production details or secondary flavors, what truly unites Scandinavians around aquavit is the culture that surrounds the drink and how it weaves its way through daily life in northern Europe.

HOW TO DRINK, SERVE, AND ENJOY AQUAVIT

There is no wrong way to enjoy aquavit. It is consumed at room temperature or frozen. It is consumed on its own, alongside beer, or with food. It is shot quickly or it is sipped, and we can confirm that it has been consumed directly from the bottle. The only rule for drinking aquavit is that it's consumed to create good memories. We find that it's best to keep a bottle of aquavit alongside a couple of small glasses in the freezer, ready to be poured in a moment of celebration. Keeping it in the freezer reduces the sensation of alcohol on the palate and makes the drink more approachable to everyone. A short glass can be sipped or shot with a "Cheers!" (also "Skål," "Skál," "Skol," or "Kippis").

Another easy way to enjoy aquavit is to keep a bottle on your bar to drink with a meal, served neat or on the rocks, however you enjoy. The savory flavor profile combined with the proof of aquavit are particularly friendly to fatty foods (such as fish packed in oil or cured meat) or foods high in acidity (such as pickles).

OTHER HERBAL LIQUEURS

Aquavit is just one of the many European spirits with rich histories, distinct flavors, and passionate fan bases. There are entire books written about some of these products, but here is a primer on two we encourage you to try if you haven't already.

Fernet-Branca is an Italian amaro that traces its roots back to Milan. To say it's an acquired taste is perhaps a bit generous. It is very dark in color, with a hint of yellow around the edges that belies the huge amounts of saffron that go into the recipe. It has a bracing bitterness from gentian, a soft sensation from aloe and chamomile, and a subtle menthol finish. In American drinking culture, Fernet-Branca has become a calling card in the restaurant industry. It is widely acknowledged that its popularity started in San Francisco, with bartenders first challenging each other to drink it and quickly becoming enamored with it and calling for shots whenever the desire arose. That love has since spread around the country to bartenders, cooks, and bussers in every city and town; chances are if you've already tried Fernet-Branca, you were introduced by a friend who works in the service industry. If you're wondering what to do besides sip it straight, try one of our most popular recipes using it, the Saffron Sour (page 140).

The Italians have a way with lower-proof bitters, and Cynar is one of our favorites to mix with or to drink straight. It is a mellower amaro than Fernet-Branca in both flavor and proof and derives some of its uniqueness from artichoke, which is used as one of the flavoring agents. For a Cynar recipe, try the Trident (page 136) or In the Pines (page 139).

THE NORSEMAN

We are quite proud of this drink. It not only tastes delicious but also brings a new and fun take on some of our favorite things. When we started developing this drink, it was an aquavit Old Fashioned—simple and good but unexciting. The breakthrough came when we decided to fat-wash the aquavit with brown butter. This drink really shows off what aquavit can taste like, pairing caraway and brown butter with bitters and a green apple garnish.

YIELD: 1 DRINK ✧ **GLASS: CHILLED DOUBLE OLD FASHIONED**

---

2 ounces Brown Butter–Washed Aquavit (recipe follows)

2 dashes Angostura bitters

1 teaspoon rich simple syrup (see page 191)

Green apple slices, for garnish

Combine the aquavit, bitters, and syrup in a chilled double old fashioned glass.

Add ice, stir, and garnish with the apple slices.

BROWN BUTTER–WASHED AQUAVIT

Fat washing is a technique that is very similar to any other type of infusion, but as the name suggests, it uses extremely fatty products. Spirits are allowed to rest with high-fat items (such as brown butter, bacon, or heavy cream) for six to eight hours, getting agitated every hour. This allows the spirit to take on flavors from the fatty product. The fats are then removed from the spirit by placing the entire mixture in the freezer until the fats solidify. The fats are then strained off, leaving just the flavored spirit behind.

YIELD: 750ML

---

1 (750ml) bottle aquavit (we use Krogstad Festlig from House Spirits in Portland, Oregon)

3 tablespoons unsalted butter

Heat the butter in a small skillet over low heat. Once it's melted, continue to heat and stir until browned. Immediately remove the skillet from the heat and pour the butter into a glass mixing bowl.

Once the butter has cooled a bit, add the aquavit to the bowl. Allow mixture to rest for 6 to 8 hours at room temperature, agitating regularly, about once an hour. Freeze the mixture until the fats solidify, and then strain off the solids with a fine strainer or cheesecloth. Keep in a clean, sealed bottle in the freezer. We've found it stays good indefinitely, until it is consumed.

FINNISH NAIL

It is a risky proposition to play with well-executed classic cocktails. The Rusty Nail has always been one of our favorite after-dinner drinks, and we've added a small amount of our cardamom-coriander syrup to our preferred specifications on a Rusty Nail, bringing Scandinavian flavors along. It is a great accompaniment to a roaring fire and a cigar.

YIELD: 1 DRINK ⁓ **GLASS: CHILLED DOUBLE OLD FASHIONED**

2 ounces blended Scotch

½ ounce Drambuie

¼ ounce Hunt + Alpine Cardamom-Coriander Syrup (see page 74)

Lemon peel, for garnish

Combine the Scotch, Drambuie, and syrup in a mixing glass.

Add ice to fill the glass. Stir for 20 to 30 seconds.

Strain into a chilled double old fashioned glass with a large ice cube. Garnish with a lemon peel.

HUNT + ALPINE
DIY AQUAVIT

One of the most frustrating parts of opening Hunt + Alpine was dealing with loads of red tape from the city and state governments, especially when it came to the liquor selection available to consumers in our state. When Prohibition was repealed by the passage of the Twenty-First Amendment, states were allowed to create whatever distribution system they saw fit. In Maine, our government chose to create a state-controlled distribution systems instead of opting for some blend of private distributors licensed by the state. That state control of our liquor distribution exists to this day. For any importer, distributor, or producer of liquor to sell their product in Maine, they must fill out pages of paperwork.

Before Hunt + Alpine opened, there were very few businesses that were looking for specific products or brands that weren't mainstream—there wasn't a single mezcal available, and the aquavits that were listed had not been kept in stock for years. That meant we had to craft an infusion that would recreate aquavit to be able to serve what we were hoping to use as a signature product for our bar. Here you will find our house recipe, which we still use to this day. It's not quite as refined as some of the commercially available products, but we're happy with the recipe, as it brings a strong herbal component that complements dishes with big flavor.

YIELD: 750ML

2 teaspoons caraway seeds

1 teaspoon coriander seeds

2 teaspoons green cardamom pods, crushed

2 black cardamom pods, crushed

½ teaspoon anise seed

1 (750ml) bottle vodka

2 orange twists

Preheat your oven to 450°F.

Spread the cardamom pods and caraway, coriander, and anise seeds on a small rimmed baking sheet and place in the oven for 10 minutes, or until fragrant, shaking the pan occasionally. Remove the pan from the oven and allow to cool in a bowl. Using a spice grinder or the back of a heavy frying pan, roughly crush all the spices.

Pour the vodka into a container large enough to hold the entire bottle worth. Add the spices and orange twists, squeezing the peels to release their oils. Cover the container and allow to steep at room temperature overnight, or at least 12 hours.

After steeping, pour the liquid through a coffee filter–lined colander into another large container and discard all the solids. Bottle the aquavit and store it in the freezer. This keeps indefinitely.

TRIDENT

When you try enough drink recipes, you will come across ones that you just smack yourself for not thinking of beforehand. For instance, this brilliant aquavit take on an Negroni smartly dries the drink out by using fino sherry instead of sweet vermouth and keeps the herbal notes low with the artichoke-based Cynar. All of the flavors are tied together with a couple of dashes of peach bitters. It is a relief to know that this drink was created before we were working in bars and restaurants by Robert Hess, a cocktail enthusiast who is part of a small cadre who laid the foundation for much of the modern cocktail movement, exchanging information and ideas online well before most of us had heard of the internet. When a guest is looking to try something with aquavit, we often turn to this cocktail; it highlights how approachable and interesting aquavit can be.

YIELD: 1 DRINK ～ **GLASS: CHILLED COCKTAIL**

1 ounce aquavit

1 ounce fino sherry

1 ounce Cynar

2 dashes peach bitters

Lemon peel, for garnish

Combine the aquavit, sherry, Cynar, and bitters in a mixing glass.

Add ice to fill the glass, and then stir for 20 to 30 seconds.

Strain into a chilled cocktail glass. Garnish with a lemon twist.

IN THE PINES

Bartending often can be a prolonged career stop before pursuing other creative endeavors— we've worked with people who have gone on to be musicians, photographers, artists, and writers. One of our former bartenders at Hunt + Alpine, Chris Buerkle, always had his sights set on nursing school. It was a sad-yet-joyous day when we learned that he had been accepted to the program he wanted to attend. We were thrilled for him but disappointed that we wouldn't get to spend more late nights working alongside him. Thankfully Chris left us with a number of spectacular drinks, including this simple-to-execute riff on a Negroni that uses an herbal liqueur and an Italian digestif in place of sweet vermouth and Campari. With Maine being the Pine Tree State, this cocktail feels right at home on a cool evening or after a walk in the woods.

YIELD: 1 DRINK   GLASS: CHILLED DOUBLE OLD FASHIONED

1 ounce St. George Terroir gin

1 ounce Zirbenz Stone Pine Liqueur

1 ounce Cynar

4–6 drops Woodland Bitters (made by Portland Bitter Project), or similar

Lemon peel, for garnish

Combine the gin, Zirbenz, Cynar, and bitters in a mixing glass.

Add ice to fill the glass, and then stir for 20 to 30 seconds.

Strain into a chilled double old fashioned glass with a large ice cube. Garnish with a lemon twist.

SAFFRON SOUR

In our younger years, we enjoyed the taste of Fernet-Branca. In fact, we still do, though nei-ther of us drinks it nearly as much as we used to. (For more on the spirit, see page 128.) When Andrew was younger, using Fernet-Branca as the primary ingredient in a balanced and deli-cious cocktail was a challenge he frequently took on and often failed. When we were devel-oping the menu for Hunt + Alpine, the challenge was revisited, and instead of using equally strong and intense ingredients, we softened its edges with fresh lime juice and egg whites and tied everything together with saffron syrup made by our friends at Royal Rose. The result is no longer on the menu, but it's still a drink we find ourselves making by request nearly every week. It's an intriguing mix of bitter and complex balanced with the bright, bracing acid of lime and rounded out with the texture provided by egg whites.

YIELD: 1 DRINK ❧ **GLASS: CHILLED COCKTAIL**

1½ ounces Fernet-Branca

¾ ounce fresh lime juice

½ ounce Royal Rose Saffron Syrup (available seasonally online)

1 teaspoon rich simple syrup (see page 191)

½ ounce egg white

Combine the Fernet-Branca, lime juice, saffron syrup, rich simple syrup, and egg white in a mixing tin.

Fill the tin with ice, cap it, and shake hard for 20 seconds.

Uncap the tin, and fine strain the contents into the empty top of the tin.

When you're finished straining, dump all the spent ice from the bottom, transfer the liquid back to the tin, cap, and shake without ice for 10 seconds. This further emulsifies the ingredients to ensure that the drink doesn't separate when served. Pour the drink into a chilled cocktail glass.

PICKLED SMELT (AND OTHER FISH)

Pickled fish is a love or hate sort of thing. We're proud to say that our recipe, which we've been using at Hunt + Alpine almost since we've opened, has converted many haters. This is also a great recipe to introduce pickled fish to those who haven't tried it; it uses a milder fish and isn't overpowering in flavor (though you can get more adventurous if you'd like). Serve it up with some homemade aquavit (see page 135) and you have a classic Scandinavian combination that we keep going back to year after year.

YIELD: ABOUT 4 TO 5 PINT JARS

- 2½ cups pickling/canning salt
- 3 pounds dressed smelt
- 3 cups distilled white vinegar
- 1½ cups sugar
- ½ cup white wine
- ¼ cup pickling spice
- 2 bay leaves
- 1 tablespoon whole allspice
- 1 tablespoon whole cloves
- 1 cup thinly sliced white onion
- 4 lemon slices

Combine the salt with 1 gallon water in a large nonreactive container. Add the smelt and let it soak, covered, in the refrigerator for 12 hours. Remove the fish and rinse it for 5 minutes under cold running water.

Combine the vinegar, sugar, wine, pickling spice, bay leaves, allspice, cloves, onions, and lemon slices in a pot that's large enough to fit all the smelt. Bring the mixture to a boil, add the smelt, and simmer on low for about 10 minutes. If the smelt is fresh, simmer it in the pickling liquid for less time—about 5 minutes. Remove the pot from the heat and cool the fish and liquid to room temperature (this will take about an hour).

Once the fish cools, pack it in 3 to 4 pint-size mason jars, using care to only transfer a small amount of the allspice, bay leaves, cloves, onion, and lemon to each jar. Strain the remaining pickling liquid and pour enough into the jars so that the smelt is covered by liquid.

Hand tighten the jar lids and let rest, refrigerated, for 1 week. The fish will keep in the refrigerator for up to 1 month.

CHAPTER 7

ENTERTAINING IN THE SNOW

We moved to Maine in the dead of winter—December 14, to be exact. Our first place, an airy loft apartment in which we would eventually host our "Hush, Hush" popups, was a block off Casco Bay and just a five-minute walk from the heart of Portland. From here, we watched blizzards roll in and cross-country skiers commute to work. We experienced Portland winters firsthand. It was during one of our first blizzards together that we came up with the idea to open Hunt + Alpine.

Once Hunt + Alpine was open, we watched winter roll in and out from the bar's large windows overlooking Tommy's Park, a small park right across the street. We've seen everyone from skiers and snowmobilers to reporters from the Weather Channel make use of that park. Here, like almost everywhere in Maine and all around the north, the place changes with the season. Tourists are harder to find, the landscape is covered in various shades of white and brown instead of green, and a snow-deadened quiet descends upon everything. Every winter there are still late nights when we sit at the bar and drink whatever our cocktail of choice is, look out the large windows that overlook the park, and watch the snow fall silently. It is a magical sight.

THE PLEASURES OF EMBRACING THE COLD

Mainers are some of the best people to be around in the winter. We find ourselves outside almost as much in the winter as we do in the summer. When you have the right tools and mindset, entertaining outside in the snow is pretty amazing.

For Briana, it would be a lie to say she has always embraced the cold. She had to learn how to enjoy the cold weather because in the Pacific Northwest, where she grew up, winters were wet and mild. Luckily, Maine is an incredible source of inspiration in the winter, so learning to adapt hasn't been that hard. Andrew grew up in Vermont, another incredible place in the winter, so he is right at home building fires, skiing, ice fishing, and snowshoeing.

One of our first winters here in Maine, before we had kids, we went sledding with a group of friends. Everyone was bundled up in coats, hats, mittens, boots, and scarves, but we were the only two who brought a thermos full of a warm cocktail—a drink that ended up being the perfect post-sledding warmup as we all headed to dinner.

IN COLD BLOOD

This cocktail was created for the Portland Museum of Art's annual Contemporaries Winter Bash, but the In Cold Blood quickly went on our own menu as well. The perfect way to drink this cocktail is standing outside in the middle of winter next to a big bonfire. In fact, this is a drink that works incredibly well in a flask. Just set the flask in the snow in between sips to keep it nice and cold. Or, if you must, you can also drink this one cozied up inside.

YIELD: 1 DRINK ⁓ GLASS: CHILLED DOUBLE OLD FASHIONED

1 ounce rye whiskey

1 ounce Cynar

1 ounce sweet vermouth

Lemon disk, for garnish

Maldon salt, or similar, for garnish
(pretzel salt works as well)

Combine the whiskey, Cynar, and vermouth in a chilled double old fashioned glass over a big ice cube. Stir.

Garnish with a lemon disk cut from the side to include a small amount of pulp and plenty of peel. The goal is to get a dribble of juice along with the oils when you express it over the drink. Finish with a heavy pinch of salt.

NOTE: *At this point, if you want to transfer it to a flask, go right ahead!*

THINGS WE USE TO STAY WARM

- Wool blankets (preferably Pendleton)
- L.L. Bean slippers
- Scotch (something smoky from the Islay region) or mezcal—anything that reminds us of other climates
- Thick-knit wool socks
- Firewood
- Music from Bill Withers, Loretta Lynn, Spencer Albee, and Beyoncé
- Hooded sweatshirts (we have enough to clothe a small army thanks to liquor brands, old jobs, and our alma mater)
- Tandem Coffee
- Pulla fresh from the oven (see page 170)
- A slideshow of our last trip to Palm Springs (for moments of true desperation)

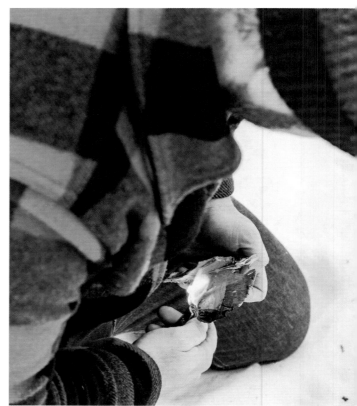

HOW TO BUILD A BONFIRE

A well-built fire is comforting and fun, and it provides a center point for gathering when you're outside in the snow. It's one of those perfect pieces to a party that everyone enjoys. Adults can cozy up to one for warmth, and children can build s'mores. Done right it makes a commanding centerpiece. There is an art to building a great fire, but once you do it, the rest of the night will come together easily.

This should go without saying, but just so we've said it: Always build a fire in a safe spot, and make sure you have enough water on hand to extinguish your fire thoroughly when you're done. It takes about twenty minutes to safely put out a fire, so plan for this time. There are many techniques for building a great fire, depending on the size. We have found the two methods that follow to be the best for our purposes.

ELEMENTS OF A GREAT FIRE

TINDER: This can be anything from newspaper to dry leaves. It catches fire quickly and helps get your wood burning.

KINDLING: These smaller pieces of wood are part of the foundation for a solid burn. They will help get larger logs going.

FIREWOOD: These larger, dry pieces of wood will burn longer and keep the fire roaring.

SMALL FIRE: LINCOLN-LOG STYLE

Building any fire is essentially the same in that you're going to be starting a tiny fire and building it into the appropriate size. For a small fire in a pit, fireplace, or campsite ring, this is a simple and great option for a fire you can cook over. You will essentially be building a small fire within a roughly built log cabin consisting of pairs of logs stacked on top of one another at 90 degree angles with room between them for air to pass through.

Start out by gathering all of the necessary items for your fire: small tinder (tiny branches, wood shavings, leaves, or paper), kindling, and larger wood pieces. (Don't forget the matches.) The

Continued on next page

largest wood pieces should be about 2 feet in length, though it is okay to go up to 3 feet. In the center of your fire pit, lay two of your smaller wood pieces parallel. Leave just enough space between the two logs to allow your logs to cross the gap comfortably at a right angle. Before building another layer, place as much tinder as can fit in a small pile at the center of the two logs. Build the second layer of your logs perpendicular to the first. On top of your small burn pile at the center of your cabin, place more dry tinder material. Then build a third layer of perpendicular logs. Light the dry material at the bottom of your cabin and allow it to catch more of the tinder on fire. Slowly but continuously add more dry tinder in larger and larger pieces. The longer you feed this fire, the more the logs on the exterior will catch and start to burn.

Once your walls have sufficiently lit, you can continuously add layers of logs to the fire, building it up and creating a small shelf for a frying pan or cooking grate. Allow enough material to burn to create a very hot pile of embers at the base of the fire before using the fire for cooking. Enjoy this fire all night by simply adding logs to the top of it as the fire starts to mellow out. Timing all depends on the heat of the fire and the dryness of the wood. We usually try to add a new log whenever the last few that were added are still solid but well charred.

BONFIRE: TEEPEE STYLE

The same basic principles you use for a small fire apply to creating a teepee-style fire: you'll start tiny and build slowly. With this technique, you will be building a fire that has the potential to vary in size from something to warm your hands to an enormous bonfire. Again, gather all of the necessary items for your fire: matches, small tinder (tiny branches, wood shavings, leaves, or paper), kindling, and larger wood pieces. If you want to build a larger fire, the wood pieces should be cut in longer lengths, around 3 to 6 feet long.

Start by creating a tripod with three of the sturdiest pieces, with the base of each piece well within your designated fire ring or burn area. At the center of the base of the tripod, place dry, leafy material and small pieces of tinder. Before lighting the dry fuel, stack more pieces around the tripod, being careful not to collapse it. The goal is to support the structure. Light the fire and grow it by carefully adding increasingly larger pieces of tinder until the tripod structure is lit. Stand back and enjoy. Continue to tend to the fire by placing additional wood around the standing tripod to ensure its structural integrity. This method can be used to make truly enormous fires; be safe!

FOXY BOXER

Stupid simple to make, the only difficulty with this drink is sourcing Moxie (see box below). It is essential to the Foxy Boxer, but it can be a hard soda to track down outside of Maine. The combination of two offbeat, bitter ingredients, however, makes for a really tasty cocktail. (Perhaps it's because both Moxie and Fernet-Branca are both bittered with gentian root.) In any case, this unusual combination just works. We like to drink this while cracking open a tin or two of sardines in front of our fireplace and playing backgammon. It's the perfect drink for a night at home once the kids are in bed.

NOTE: *If you are hosting a crowd, we see no reason not to just set the Fernet-Branca and Moxie on the table and let your guests serve themselves. It's almost impossible to screw this one up.*

YIELD: 1 DRINK ❧ **GLASS: DOUBLE OLD FASHIONED**

1½ ounces Fernet-Branca   **4 ounces Moxie**

Pour the Fernet-Branca into a double old fashioned glass and add ice. Fill to the top with Moxie. That's it!

MOXIE

If you have ever been to New England or met someone from Maine and had a conversation about soda, there is a good chance you've heard of Moxie. Moxie is a uniquely New England soda that has been around for over a century. It is actually where the English word *moxie*, meaning "courage, spunk, or spirit," comes from.

Moxie is more bitter and less sweet than typical colas produced today. It is bittered by gentian root (the same ingredient that makes many bitters and digestifs so bitter), and the soda was traditionally sold as a medicinal tonic. In the late 1800s, it was sold under the name "Moxie Nerve Food." While the drink's ties to the state of Maine aren't a monopoly (the drink was invented in Massachusetts and is currently produced by a company in New Hampshire), its identity rests predominantly in Maine. It is the official soft drink of Maine, and for over twenty-five years an annual festival has been held in the Maine town of Lisbon Falls, celebrating all things Moxie.

As a cultural touchstone, Moxie has inspired and been a comfort to many a Mainer. The drinks and names developed around Moxie stand second only to Allen's Coffee Flavored Brandy (see page 164). As a cocktail ingredient, Moxie is a wonderful alternative to the sickly sweet sodas and colas you typically find, and it allows you to find balance in a cocktail as well as bring something unique to the glass.

MEXICO, MAINE

Did you know there's actually a town in Maine called Mexico? This cocktail is what came to our minds as we envisioned a marriage of Mexico and Maine. It's based on the strong flavors of Allen's Coffee Flavored Brandy (see page 164) and mezcal. Thus, you have the iconic spirits of Maine and Mexico! The tequila and agave help balance out the bitterness that can result from Allen's, and they stick with the theme. We've found this is a drink that's made for cold weather. It's a friend of fried food and won't ever say no to a campfire.

YIELD: 1 DRINK ❧ **GLASS: CHILLED DOUBLE OLD FASHIONED**

1½ ounces El Jimador Blanco

½ ounce mezcal (we use Del Maguey Vida)

½ ounce Allen's Coffee Flavored Brandy

1 teaspoon agave syrup

6 dashes coffee bitters (there are many great ones on the market, but we use Coastal Root, made right here in Portland)

Orange peel, for garnish

Add the El Jimador, mezcal, Allen's, agave, and bitters to a well-chilled double old fashioned glass.

Add a large ice cube, and then stir for 20 to 30 seconds. Garnish with an expressed orange peel.

BUTTERSCOTCH BUDINO WITH PISTACHIO PRALINE

Budino, the Italian word for custard or pudding, is a rich, creamy dish. The flavors in this recipe are an ideal companion to strong winter drinks and hearty meals. We've found it is rich enough to stand up to heavier cocktails (such as In Cold Blood, an Old Fashioned, or even a shot of aquavit) but still delicate enough to not be an overly filling dessert.

YIELD: 6 SERVINGS

1½ cups brown sugar	¼ cup cornstarch
3 cups heavy cream	6 tablespoons unsalted butter
1½ cups whole milk	2 teaspoons kosher salt
1 egg	2 tablespoons dark rum
3 egg yolks	1 tablespoon vanilla extract

In a large, heavy-bottomed pot, combine the brown sugar and ½ cup water. Cook over medium-high heat until the mixture turns a dark caramel color but does not burn, approximately 5 minutes. The sugar should be mildly fragrant and the mixture syrupy.

Slowly pour in the cream and milk, stirring constantly as you combine the dairy with the caramel. Continue to cook over medium-high heat until the caramel is completely dissolved in the liquid. Remove the pot from the heat and set aside.

In a medium mixing bowl, whisk the egg, egg yolks, and cornstarch together. Temper the hot liquid into the egg mixture by slowly adding a cup of the hot cream into the eggs while continually stirring. Mix thoroughly, and then add the egg mixture back into the pot with the remaining hot liquid and cook over medium heat until it thickens enough to coat the back of a spoon.

Remove the pot from the heat and add the butter, salt, rum, and vanilla. Stir to combine. Taste and adjust the flavorings, if needed. Once it is to your taste, carefully pour the mixture through a sieve into a heatproof container and chill in the fridge for 2 hours or until cool.

To serve, portion into small bowls. Garnish with Pistachio Praline (recipe follows).

PISTACHIO PRALINE

YIELD: 2 CUPS

½ cup raw shelled pistachios

½ teaspoon cinnamon

Pinch Aleppo or Korean chili powder

Dash kosher salt

1½ cups sugar

Maldon salt, for sprinkling

Canola oil, for greasing

Preheat your oven to 450ºF. Place the pistachios on a rimmed baking sheet and bake for approximately 5 minutes. You'll want to check on them frequently and stir them from time to time to ensure even cooking. The goal here is a light toast, so cook until just fragrant and starting to change color. Once the pistachios are done, toss them in a bowl with the cinnamon, chili powder, and kosher salt.

Lightly grease a medium-size heavy-bottomed pot. Combine the sugar and 1½ cups water in the pot and set over high heat. Line a baking sheet with a silicone baking mat or parchment paper and grease it well, and then set it aside. When the sugar mixture comes to a boil, cover the pot with its lid for 3 minutes. Remove the lid, reduce the heat to medium, and continue cooking until the sugar starts to caramelize and turn brown. Once the sugar is a light- to medium-brown color, immediately stir in the pistachios. We've found that lightly buttering a spatula helps with this step. It will help you stir in the nuts with less sticking.

Once the nuts are evenly distributed, pour the mixture out onto your prepared greased baking sheet. Sprinkle the Maldon over the top and let cool at room temperature for about 30 minutes, or until the mixture hardens.

Break into pieces and serve. This keeps, covered, at room temperature for 1 week.

CHOCOLATE BUDINO WITH WALNUT BRITTLE

While we absolutely love Butterscotch Budino (see page 156), there are always requests from the chocolate lovers of the world. For those folks, our team at Hunt + Alpine worked this recipe into the menu one autumn. It's delicious any time of year but particularly when you're feeling extra decadent. It is rich, thick, and incredibly smooth. Pair it with a glass of sherry, champagne, or our Green Eyes cocktail (page 32).

YIELD: 6 SERVINGS

- **1½ cups brown sugar**
- **3 cups heavy cream**
- **1½ cups whole milk**
- **1 egg**
- **3 egg yolks**
- **¼ cup cornstarch**

- **¼ cup cocoa powder**
- **4 cups chocolate chips**
- **6 tablespoons unsalted butter**
- **2 teaspoons kosher salt**
- **½ teaspoon ground black cardamom**
- **2 tablespoons brandy**

In a large, heavy-bottomed pot, combine the brown sugar and ½ cup water. Cook over medium-high heat until the mixture turns a dark caramel color but does not burn. The sugar should be mildly fragrant and the mixture syrupy.

Slowly pour in the cream and milk, stirring constantly as you combine the dairy with the caramel. Continue to cook over medium-high heat until the caramel is completely dissolved in the liquid. Remove the pot from the heat and set aside.

In a medium mixing bowl, whisk the egg, egg yolks, cocoa, and cornstarch together. Temper the hot liquid into the egg mixture by slowly adding a cup of the hot cream into the eggs while continually stirring. Mix thoroughly, and then add the egg mixture back into the pot with the hot liquid. Once it's fully incorporated, add the chocolate chips. Cook over medium heat until the mixture thickens enough to coat the back of a spoon.

Add the butter, salt, and black cardamom. Stir to combine. Taste and adjust the flavorings, if needed. Once it is to your taste, carefully pour the mixture through a sieve into a heatproof container and chill in the fridge for 2 hours, or until cool. Stir in the brandy once the mixture is fully cooled.

To serve, portion into small bowls. Garnish with the Shio Koji Whipped Cream and Walnut Brittle (recipes follow).

SHIO KOJI WHIPPED CREAM

YIELD: 1 CUP

1 cup heavy cream

¼ cup sugar

6 tablespoons shio koji solids

NOTE: *Shio koji is a fermented rice solid that is used in Japanese cooking to bring umami flavors to a dish. It is available at specialty stores and online.*

Combine the cream, sugar, and shio koji in a mixing bowl or in the bowl of a stand mixer. Whisk on medium speed until soft peaks form, approximately 5 minutes.

WALNUT BRITTLE

YIELD: APPROXIMATELY 3 CUPS (SAVE WHATEVER IS LEFT OVER FOR SNACKING)

1½ cups shelled walnuts

Pinch Korean chili powder

Dash kosher salt

1½ cups sugar

Maldon sea salt, for sprinkling

Canola oil, for greasing

Preheat your oven to 450°F. Place the walnuts on a rimmed baking sheet and bake for approximately 5 minutes. You'll want to check on them frequently and stir them from time to time to ensure even cooking. The goal here is a light toast, so cook until just fragrant and starting to change color. Once the walnuts are done, toss them in a bowl with the chili powder and kosher salt.

Lightly grease a medium-size heavy-bottomed pot. Combine the sugar and 1½ cups water in the pot and set over high heat. Line a baking sheet with a silicone baking mat or parchment paper and grease it well, and then set it aside. When the sugar mixture comes to a boil, cover the pot with its lid for 3 minutes. Remove the lid, reduce the heat to medium, and continue cooking until the sugar starts to caramelize and turn brown. Once the sugar is a light- to medium-brown color, immediately stir in the walnuts. We've found that lightly buttering a spatula helps with this step. It will help you stir in the nuts with less sticking.

Once the nuts are evenly distributed, pour the mixture out onto your prepared greased baking sheet. Sprinkle the Maldon over the top and let cool at room temperature for about 30 minutes, or until the mixture hardens.

Break into pieces and serve. This keeps, covered, at room temperature for 1 week.

CLAMS WITH ABSINTHE AND BOTTARGA

This recipe embodies so much of what we value in our food. It has a strong sense of place and represents local seafood very well. Yet it's an easy dish to learn and requires minimum cleanup as well. With no sacrifice to flavor, you'll dirty only one pan! We think it's best when served with a dark beer and some warm, crusty bread to sop up the buttery broth.

YIELD: 2 SERVINGS

- ½ **pound Manila clams**
- **3 tablespoons cold water**
- **1½ teaspoons sriracha**
- **Lemon twist**
- **4 tablespoons unsalted butter, at room temperature**

- **Pinch ground pink pepper**
- **Approximately 1 tablespoon grated bottarga (cured fish roe), for garnish**
- **3 pumps absinthe from an atomizer (see page 17)**

Wash the clams well, making sure to remove any dirt or grit.

In a medium-size pan, add the clams, water, lemon twist, and sriracha. Cook over high heat until the mixture begins to boil.

Add the butter and watch the pot. As the clams begin to open, remove each one from the pan with tongs and place it in your serving dish. After all the clams have cooked and been transferred to the serving dish, pour the sauce over the clams.

Sprinkle with the pink pepper and bottarga. Mist the clams 3 times with the absinthe and serve.

FISH FRY

The only thing better than standing out in the cold and pulling in smelt from a hole in the ice is bringing that smelt home and eating it. We prefer to cook our smelt as soon as possible after catching it. Why refrigerate it when you can eat it at its best? For a winter feast, serve this with root vegetables that have been chopped into big chunks and roasted with olive oil and salt.

YIELD: 8 SERVINGS

1 egg, beaten

½ cup whole milk

1 cup all-purpose flour

1 teaspoon red pepper flakes or cayenne pepper

1 tablespoon kosher salt

Pinch black pepper

3 pounds smelt or similar small fish such as mackerel or sardines (if you're buying these from your local fishmonger, have them clean the fish and remove the heads)

1 cup peanut oil, or enough for frying

NOTE: *We love the flavor of frying with peanut oil, but if you are worried about peanut allergies, feel free to substitute another oil. If you use a more neutral oil, you can add a little flavor by throwing in a crushed garlic clove at the beginning to flavor the oil (remove it before it begins to burn).*

In a small bowl, mix together the egg and milk. Set aside. In another bowl, mix together the flour, red pepper flakes, salt, and pepper, and transfer the mixture to a shallow baking dish. This will make it easier to dredge the fish.

Pat the smelt dry with paper towels. Run them through the egg and milk mixture, and then dredge them in the flour mixture. In large batches, dredge the fish and place on a plate, ready to be fried.

Once the smelt have all been dredged, it's time to get the oil ready to fry. We like to use a cast-iron skillet, but you can use any pan that's suitable for frying. Heat the peanut oil until it's glistening but not smoking, approximately 350°F.

Add the fish a few at a time and cook until browned on one side, and then flip to cook the other side. Since the fish are small, it shouldn't take more than about 30 seconds per side.

Place the fried fish on a paper-towel-lined plate until all the smelt are cooked. Once all the smelt are ready, transfer them onto a serving platter (with the roasted vegetables, if you're making them, or other accompaniments). Eat them whole while still hot!

ALLEN'S COFFEE FLAVORED BRANDY

Many cities and states have a locally famous food or ingredient virtually impossible to find outside their borders (except that which is smuggled away). In Maine we have Allen's Coffee Brandy. Allen's is a blend of coffee flavoring with sugar and a neutral spirit. It clocks in at 30% alcohol by volume (ABV), though until recently it was also produced at 40% ABV. Despite actually being made in Massachusetts, Allen's finds most of its consumer base in Maine. Flavor-wise, Allen's is pretty straightforward, with a nose of slightly burnt coffee syrup, tasting of strong coffee, with the sugar coating the palate in a way that disguises much of the alcohol, and a finish that is both pleasant and a bit copper-like at the same time.

According to MS Walker, the company that produces Allen's, the popularity of their coffee brandy started with Maine fishermen looking for a morning pick-me-up in their morning coffee. It was the perfect warming ingredient in a hot cup of coffee on a cold morning when they'd push off from the docks at 4 a.m. From there, Allen's came off the water and into the glasses of nearly every Mainer, which is not an exaggeration—according to numbers independently verified by the State of Maine's Bureau of Alcoholic Beverages, Allen's Coffee Brandy outsells every other spirit in the state by a staggering amount. Some quick, back-of-the-napkin math shows that one in every seven bottles of alcohol sold in Maine is Allen's Coffee Brandy. Our state tracks sales by each size of bottle of each product, and Allen's makes the Top 10 list four times—the one liter, the 750 milliliter, the handle (1.75 liter), and the pint.

Most of the Allen's poured is served at home or in bars, mixed with milk, and classically called a Sombrero. But in Maine it has taken on a multitude of other nicknames, most of which are not fit for print. However, we at Hunt + Alpine have been fascinated by the product and have developed entire menus around it, including the Mexico, Maine (see page 155). Additionally, we have replaced all other coffee brandies with Allen's and make everything from a White Russian to our version of the Espresso Martini (see page 167) with Allen's, exclusively.

Our embrace of such a culturally ingrained product has thrilled many Mainers who come in to check out what we're doing. After sitting at the bar and flipping through the cocktail menu and scanning our backbar, we'll often hear, "This is great and all, but I bet you don't have Allen's back there anywhere." Every time, we can grin and reach for it in our well and explain that it's the only coffee liqueur that we carry. Then we can offer them the traditional Allen's and milk, or one of our house drinks with Allen's. And every time they love it, we hope we've made another guest for life.

ESPRESSO MARTINI

Taking on a classic recipe and trying to make a riff or variation on it that's even better is a daunting task. When it comes to the Manhattan or Negroni, we'll almost always drink a well-made classic twice over a house variation. Still, there are exceptions. Our intention with this drink was never to update or change it but instead to be able to produce a consistently great drink in a space that doesn't have an espresso machine while highlighting a phenomenally popular local product in Allen's Coffee Flavored Brandy (see page 164). We think the solution we developed has made this drink as good as the original, and some of our favorite and most respected peers feel it may be even better. For a deep dive, see page 169.

YIELD: 1 DRINK ⁓ **GLASS: CHILLED COCKTAIL**

2 ounces Sweetened Coffee Concentrate (recipe follows)

1 ounce Plantation 3 Stars white rum

1 ounce Allen's Coffee Flavored Brandy

Add the coffee concentrate, rum, and Allen's to a mixing tin.

Add ice to the tin, cap, and shake hard for 30 to 45 seconds.

Fine strain into a chilled cocktail glass. Enjoy immediately.

SWEETENED COFFEE CONCENTRATE

The way we make this requires the use of a Filtron device, though making a strong cold brew by the same proportions can work nearly as well. The trick to the Filtron is that it is set up to minimize agitation of the coffee grounds, creating a smooth and strong brew without acidic or off flavors.

YIELD: APPROXIMATELY 36 OUNCES

1 pound coffee beans, ideally a darker espresso roast, coarsely ground

64 ounces cold water

⅓ cup sugar dissolved in ⅓ cup water (exact amount depends on your coffee yield)

Using the coffee grounds and 64 ounces cold water, make the cold brew concentrate in the Filtron according to manufacturer's instructions. Alternatively, combine the coffee and water in a large glass pitcher, cover, and allow to sit at room temperature for 12 hours. After steeping, filter twice, first using a fine-mesh filter and subsequently with a paper filter.

Weigh the amount of cold brew concentrate you made and add one-third that amount of simple syrup (equal parts sugar and water). Your batch size may differ, but we often get between 1,200 grams and 1,500 grams of coffee per batch. Stir until fully combined.

Bottle, date, and store the concentrate in the refrigerator. This will keep, refrigerated, for up to 4 weeks. You can use this in the Espresso Martini or simply dilute it with water and ice whenever you need a quick pick-me-up. (Or do as Andrew does and down a quick shot of the concentrate.)

MORE ON THE ESPRESSO MARTINI

When it comes to the Espresso Martini, it's important to know what we use as a yardstick to judge any recipe. In bars with access to freshly pulled espresso shots, we were taught and have always adhered to Dick Bradsell's recipe of 1½ ounces vodka, 1 ounce fresh espresso, and ¾ ounce coffee liqueur. The story goes that he created this recipe in 1983 for a woman who stepped up to the bar asking for a drink that would "wake me up, then f*ck me up."

At Hunt + Alpine, we don't have the space for an espresso machine, so we needed to find an easy way to prep coffee concentrate. Our friends, the owners of Tandem Coffee in Portland, Maine, suggested the use of a Filtron. If you're unfamiliar, a Filtron is a specific brand of cold brew concentrate system that produces very strong coffee concentrate over a twelve-hour soak with next to no agitation.

We started playing with Tandem's espresso blend of beans and the Filtron and discovered that we loved the coffee but it lacked the bitterness that espresso often brings to a drink. That lost balance of flavors was remedied easily, as there was no question we would also be using

Allen's Coffee Flavored Brandy. Since Allen's brings a bitter, near metallic, backbone along with a strong and sweet coffee flavor and plenty of alcohol, we just needed to adjust the ratios to our taste and find that perfect third ingredient. To round out our version, we played with nearly every base spirit imaginable (Irish whiskey, tequila, bourbon, vodka, and brandy) but eventually chose white rum because it gave the drink a rounder all-around finish without taking control of the drink. That said, if you like this drink, you should also try some variations. Make it with vodka or any other base spirit you desire. (We even have guests who swear by tequila in theirs.)

PULLA (FINNISH CARDAMOM BREAD)

Briana has many childhood memories of her grandmother and mummu making pulla—what it smelled like cooking and how heavenly it was warm out of the oven with butter. She would also sneak bites of the sweet dough before it was braided and baked. A dear family friend made her version with the addition of orange, and as adults, we've adopted that addition in our recipe. Perfect as a breakfast treat or a hearty dessert (add ice cream to a warm slice), pulla is the ultimate sweet comfort food.

While this recipe calls for 7 cups of flour, consider that the upper limit. Go lighter to start, around 4½ cups, as you want the dough to be very sticky to work with when mixing, and it will absorb additional flour when you're rolling it out. Briana's grandmother always did this, and her loaves were light and moist as opposed to dense and dry, which can happen quickly.

YIELD: 2 LOAVES

1⅓ cups warm milk

1 cup sugar

1 tablespoon crushed black cardamom pods (use a mortar and pestle to crush the pods)

2 packages (each 0.25 ounce) active dry yeast

3 eggs, beaten

½ teaspoon kosher salt

7 cups bread flour (see recipe headnote)

5 tablespoons unsalted cultured butter, melted

1 tablespoon fresh orange juice

¼ cup whole milk

½ cup lump sugar (feel free to use less or more to your taste)

Orange zest, for garnish

Combine the warm milk, sugar, cardamom, and yeast in the bowl of a stand mixer. Using the paddle attachment, stir the ingredients at medium speed for 2 minutes. If mixing by hand, add the same ingredients to a bowl and stir until evenly mixed. Let rest until foamy.

Add eggs and salt and mix at medium speed until well combined. Now add 4½ cups flour, mixing at a low speed until the dough starts forming. The dough should be very sticky but not liquid. Slowly add more flour until the dough comes together but is still moist. Beat at medium speed for about 5 minutes, or until the dough is elastic. This can be done by hand as well, ensuring the dough is evenly mixed before moving to the next step.

Attach the dough hook and knead the dough on medium speed for about 2 minutes, slowly adding the melted butter, followed by the orange juice, to the dough. Once all the butter and juice is incorporated, continue kneading for about 5 minutes. (The kneading can also be done by hand, on a lightly floured countertop.) The dough should be smooth, glossy, and still slightly sticky. Add a little more flour if it is too sticky to work with, kneading it in by hand if necessary.

Transfer the dough to a lightly buttered bowl and cover with a clean kitchen towel. Let it sit in a warm place until it has doubled in size, about 1 hour. Punch down the dough and let sit again until it has almost doubled, about 1 hour.

Once the dough has completed its second rise, preheat your oven to 375°F. Divide the dough in half, and then divide each half into 3 parts. Roll each piece into a 12-inch rope. Braid 3 ropes into a loaf, and repeat with the other 3 ropes. Brush the tops of the loaves with ¼ cup milk and then sprinkle on the lump sugar.

Bake until golden, about 20 minutes, rotating halfway through and being careful not to overbake the loaves. A cake tester should come out clean and the bread should be lightly brown when it's done.

When the bread is done, remove it from the oven and sprinkle the orange zest on top of the loaves. Let cool a few minutes before serving, but this bread is best served warm. Butter is optional.

CHAPTER 8

THE SHORT
SEASONS

One of the wonderful things about living in Maine is that we get to enjoy all four seasons. We see the seasons come and go and feel the changes each one brings. Yet being so far north means most of our time is spent in cooler, or very cold, weather. So when our brief summers finally arrive, we make the most of every second. Spending time on or near the water is one way to soak up the season. Maine has a lot of coastline—and even more if you account for the lakes and rivers inland. With so many options, you can easily find yourself on the beach or lakeside in the summer.

Even though at Hunt + Alpine our aesthetic leans Scandinavian, we can't help but bring our northern spin on warm-weather drinks and food, especially rum drinks. In fact, New England has a deep and fascinating history with rum. The area was an essential stop on the Sugar Triangle, where Caribbean sugarcane was imported and distilled into rum before heading to England for consumption. (We highly recommend Wayne Curtis's *And a Bottle of Rum* if you want to learn more about this fascinating history.) Rum and the tiki spirit inspire a few drinks that stay on our menu year round. We also bring in classics such as daiquiris and don't shy away from putting the blender to work on hot days. It's another way we keep those summer vibes going and going.

EMBRACING THE BOUNTY OF SUMMER

Twice a week we have a farmer who comes by the restaurant with his truck. He is more or less a one-man operation, and each week the produce he has will vary. In the winter we enjoy his root vegetables, but summer is when his deliveries are really exciting. From ramps and fiddleheads to carrots and peas, we can't wait to see what we'll get from week to week. Knowing how short summers here can be, we try to use as much produce as possible on our menu.

When we aren't working at the bar, we're visiting the local farmers' markets for ourselves. Then we pack the kids and dog into the car and head out to the lake or beach. While the ocean waters are generally way too cold to swim in (at least for some of us—Andrew rarely hesitates to test the temperature), the beaches here are still beautiful and kid friendly, and many of them feel incredibly private. It's just another advantage of having so much coastline and so many little islands to play around. When we are able to take these afternoons away, we always pack a picnic. That way, no matter where we end up, we have a spread ready to lay out and don't have to worry about finding a spot for a meal.

OPPK (OLD PORT PAIN KILLER)

In many of the bars Andrew worked at when he first started bartending, bartenders were loath to make blended drinks, as they were a pain to make and generally viewed as not worth the effort. If there was a blender behind the bar, it would mysteriously be out of service. Once Andrew was running the bar, however, we felt that not only would it be a challenge, but also it would be fun to have a blended cocktail on the menu. To help convince the barstaff to go along with it, we made sure to buy a blender that had preprogrammed buttons designed for professional service of blended drinks. That way they could fill the chamber up, push a button, and walk away. About thirty seconds later, the drink was done without fiddling with knobs or speeds.

This drink was developed as a blended drink for the short, hot summers of Portland's Old Port. We've taken the flavors from a Pain Killer cocktail (rum, orange, coconut) and replaced the coconut with orgeat, a traditional almond-flavored syrup popular in tiki-style drinks (see the recipe that follows). Additionally, we've added some depth to the rum profile by using a pot-stilled Jamaican rum, which tends to have strong vanilla and funky flavors, paired with a rhum agricole, which is a style produced largely in Martinique using freshly pressed sugarcane juice instead of the sugar processing byproducts that many other Caribbean island rums use.

YIELD: 1 DRINK ❧ **GLASS: COLLINS (OR A TIKI MUG IF YOU HAVE ONE)**

---

1 ounce rhum agricole

1 ounce pot-stilled Jamaican rum

1 ounce orgeat (recipe follows)

2 ounces fresh orange juice

1 ounce rich simple syrup (see page 191)

3 dashes lime bitters

Cocktail cherry and cocktail umbrella, for garnish

Combine the rhum agricole, Jamaican rum, orgeat, orange juice, syrup, and bitters in a blender.

Add 1½ cups ice, place the lid on the blender, and blend on medium high for 25 seconds. Turn the blender to high for 10 additional seconds, and then stop the blender. Timing of this truly depends on your blender's power and mixing ability. You are looking for any large ice chunks to be broken down on medium speed before increasing to the highest speed to create a consistently smooth drink.

Pour the drink into a tiki mug or similar-style glass, adding the cherry and cocktail umbrella before serving.

ORGEAT

YIELD: APPROXIMATELY 2½ CUPS

1¾ cups unsweetened almond milk

1 cup sugar

¼ teaspoon almond extract

⅛ teaspoon orange blossom water

Combine all the ingredients in a resealable container. Seal the container and shake thoroughly until fully integrated.

Once the sugar is fully dissolved, use immediately or refrigerate until you're ready to use. This will keep, refrigerated, for up to 10 days.

OUR LAKE AND BEACH PACKING LIST

In the summer, we always have a beach "go bag" in the back of our car. That way we can do last-minute beach trips without worrying about planning and packing. Most of these things stay in the car until early fall, but items such as ice, oysters, and rosé come along when we have a little time to plan. Otherwise we pick them up on our way.

- Yeti cooler
- Stanley thermos filled with a cocktail
- White or rosé wine
- Oyster knife (and oysters if we can't buy them where we're going)
- Pocket knife (Andrew has a collection of these that range from a classic Opinel to a German officer's knife)
- Wine key
- Sunscreen
- Beach towels or blankets
- 1-inch ice cubes, packed in resealable plastic bags
- Matches
- Sparklers (the 4th of July kind)
- Durable coffee mugs
- Plastic buckets and shovels for the kids
- Salt
- Lemons
- Sunshine

LATE NIGHT AT OOB

Briana, whose background is in writing for advertising and TV, was filling out dummy menu copy before Hunt + Alpine opened and made this drink name up as a joke. The original "recipe" called for "Rum, Other Things, and Shame." It quickly became something that the team loved, and they told us we had to make it come to life. Thus, the Late Night at OOB was born.

For those not already in the know, OOB is a reference to Old Orchard Beach, a party-hard beach town about thirty minutes away from Portland. It's lovingly referred to by many around here as the "Jersey Shore of Maine." Thus, we thought the drink needed to feel like tiki, salt water, wooden boardwalks, and nights that maybe you don't want to totally remember. Every so often we create a new recipe for the Late Night at OOB, and what follows are versions #1, #2, and #3. Try them all with as much or as little "shame" as you'd like.

LATE NIGHT AT OOB #1

YIELD: 1 DRINK ∾ GLASS: CHILLED DOUBLE OLD FASHIONED

1½ ounces blended white rum (we use Plantation 3 Stars)

¾ ounce fresh lime juice

½ ounce fresh pineapple juice

½ ounce falernum

1 pump absinthe from an atomizer (see page 17), Angostura bitters, a pinch of freshly grated nutmeg, and a mint sprig, for garnish

Combine the rum, lime juice, pineapple juice, and falernum in a mixing tin.

Fill the tin with ice, cap, and shake hard for 10 seconds.

Strain the drink (no need to fine strain to remove the small ice chunks here, as we find them pleasant and refreshing in this drink) and pour into a chilled double old fashioned glass.

Garnish with a spray of absinthe, a dash of bitters, a dusting of fresh nutmeg, and a mint sprig.

LATE NIGHT AT OOB #2

YIELD: 1 DRINK ⁓ **GLASS: CHILLED DOUBLE OLD FASHIONED**

1½ ounces Bimini gin or similar

¾ ounce fresh lime juice

½ ounce Cinnamon Syrup
(recipe follows)

½ ounce coconut rum (we use Clément
Mahina Coco)

1 pump absinthe from an atomizer (see
page 17), Angostura bitters, a mint sprig,
and cocktail umbrella, for garnish

NOTE: *Bimini gin is a locally produced New American–style gin. It isn't as strongly juniper flavored as most gins, which allows citrus and other botanicals to stand out.*

Combine the gin, lime juice, syrup, and rum in a mixing tin.

Fill the tin with ice, cap, and shake hard for 10 seconds.

Strain the drink (no need to fine strain to remove the small ice chunks here, as we find them pleasant and refreshing in this drink) and pour into a chilled double old fashioned glass.

Garnish with a spray of absinthe, a dash of bitters, a mint sprig, and a cocktail umbrella.

CINNAMON SYRUP

YIELD: APPROXIMATELY 2 CUPS

1½ cinnamon sticks

1 cup sugar

Preheat the oven to 450°F. Break up the cinnamon sticks and place them on a baking sheet. Roast them in the oven for 10 to 15 minutes, until fragrant.

In a small saucepan, bring 1 cup water to a boil. Turn the heat down to a simmer and add the sugar and cinnamon sticks. Stir and simmer until the sugar is completely dissolved. Turn off the heat, cover, and let cool. Steep at room temperature for 24 hours. Strain and refrigerate in a sealed container. This recipe will keep, refrigerated, for about 10 days.

LATE NIGHT AT OOB #3

YIELD: 1 DRINK ⤳ **GLASS: CHILLED DOUBLE OLD FASHIONED**

1½ ounces green chile vodka (we use St. George)

1 ounce fresh pineapple juice

½ ounce fresh lime juice

¼ ounce Cinnamon Syrup (see page 179)

¼ ounce coconut rum (we use Clément Mahina Coco)

½ ounce Pineapple Syrup (recipe follows)

Pineapple leaf and cocktail umbrella, for garnish

Combine the vodka, pineapple juice, lime juice, cinnamon syrup, rum, and pineapple syrup in a mixing tin.

Fill the tin with ice, cap, and shake hard for 10 seconds.

Strain the drink (no need to fine strain to remove the small ice chunks here, as we find them pleasant and refreshing in this drink) and pour into a chilled double old fashioned glass.

Garnish with a pineapple leaf and cocktail umbrella and serve.

PINEAPPLE SYRUP

YIELD: APPROXIMATELY 1½ CUPS

½ cup sugar

½ cup hot water

¼ of a fresh pineapple, cored and skin removed

Cut the pineapple quarter up roughly into 1-inch pieces. Set aside.

Mix the sugar and hot water together in a small mixing bowl until the sugar is dissolved. Add the pineapple pieces and stir to combine. Cover and let sit at room temperature for at least 6 hours and up to 12 hours.

Strain out the pineapple chunks through a sturdy wire mesh strainer, pressing to release as much juice as possible. Discard (or eat!) the pineapple. Use the syrup immediately or bottle and refrigerate. This recipe will keep, refrigerated, for up to 10 days.

OUR THOUGHTS ON BLENDED COCKTAILS AND DRINKS

For too long, blended drinks were almost impossible to find in most "cocktail" bars. They were considered a relic of the 1970s and 1980s, not part of the cocktail revival centered around pre-Prohibition-era drinking. However, at Hunt + Alpine, we have looked to every era to inspire and influence our cocktail menus. Very few things feel as instantly summery as a blended drink. Even though they seem simple—you just throw the ingredients in a blender and turn it on, right?—making a great blended drink does require thought. Here are a few tips we use to make blended cocktails both at the bar and at home.

THE BLENDER MATTERS: Using the right blender makes a difference. Its ability to crush ice and mix ingredients without overblending is important. Both at home and at the bar, we use Vitamix (though the model depends on the location). Note that the blender model and brand you use will determine how long you blend your drinks, so keep that in mind as you follow the recipes in this chapter. A great blender is worth the investment since it can be used for much more than just drinks.

ICE MATTERS TOO: When preparing and serving blended drinks, the shape and style of ice you use can affect the drink. It's not that there are better or worse types of ice to use (see page 48 for a further discussion on ice); all ice will chill and dilute your drinks, but you need to think about the ice you use and adjust your preparation and technique to it. If you have tray ice coming directly from the freezer, your blend times will closely reflect what we use (rock-hard 1-inch cubes). However, if you've purchased a bag of shaved ice and it's been sitting in a cooler in the sun all afternoon, you'll have something a bit looser and closer to water to start. In that instance, just a quick pulse in the blender may do the trick for the perfectly textured blended cocktail.

THINK ABOUT FLAVORS . . . AND ADD SUGAR: We are not going to delve deep into flavor science and biology, but for blended drinks, it is very helpful to understand that when you are serving a frozen drink, you are suppressing your palate's ability to pick up on flavor. When crafting a new blended drink, you should aim to use bold flavors (for example, we use some burly rums, flavorful orange juice, and a punchy almond syrup in our OPPK—see page 175). Additionally, because of the way our palates sense flavors, you cannot skimp on the sugar. Sugar, in this instance, brings out flavors that otherwise would be suppressed by the cold temperature of the frozen drink. If you're looking to create your own blended cocktail, start with twice as much sugar as you think is necessary to balance the drink, and build from there (in our experience, it will usually be closer to three times as much sugar).

SHAKEN DAIQUIRI

YIELD: 1 DRINK   ᔥ   **GLASS: CHILLED OLD FASHIONED**

2½ ounces blended white rum (we use Plantation 3 Stars)

¾ ounce fresh lime juice

½ ounce rich simple syrup (see page 191)

Add the rum, lime juice, and syrup to a mixing tin along with 2 very large (2-inch) ice cubes.

Cap the tin and shake very hard for 60 seconds. (This is longer than usual, but the large ice cubes necessitate a longer and harder shake to achieve proper temperature and dilution levels.)

Fine strain into a chilled single old fashioned glass. Drink quickly!

BLENDED DAIQUIRI

YIELD: 1 DRINK   ᔥ   **GLASS: CHILLED DOUBLE OLD FASHIONED**

1½ ounces blended white rum (we use Plantation 3 Stars)

1 ounce Jamaican pot-stilled rum (Smith & Cross brings a strong, vanilla funky flavor)

1 ounce fresh lime juice

1½ ounces rich simple syrup (see page 191)

Combine all ingredients in the pitcher of a blender.

Add 1½ cups ice, place the lid on the blender, and blend on medium-high speed for 25 seconds. Turn the blender to high for 10 additional seconds, and then stop the blender.

Pour the drink into a chilled double old fashioned glass and serve.

KESSIKEITO (SUMMER VEGETABLE STEW)

When you have short springs and summers like those in Finland and in Maine, you want to make the most of them. We think Kessikeito is a dish that celebrates summer produce with a beautiful richness and flavor. Using fresh spring and summer vegetables with a cream base, this soup tastes like it was much harder to make than it really is. We typically vary the vegetables used based on what looks the best at the farmers' market. All that is important is that they are cut in equal-size pieces and that there is a nice mix of root vegetables and greener vegetables. Enjoy it outside on a summer evening.

YIELD: 4 SERVINGS

---

2 tablespoons unsalted butter

2 tablespoons all-purpose flour

1 medium white onion, roughly chopped, or 2 cups fresh pearl onions, halved

10 fingerling or other small potatoes, cleaned but unpeeled, cut into 2-inch pieces

4 carrots, peeled and cut into equal-size slices (around ⅛ inch thick)

1 stalk celery, cut into ½-inch pieces

2 small parsnips, cut into ½-inch round pieces

1 cup whole milk

1 small head cauliflower, trimmed and cut into small florets, with most of the stalks removed

1 small head broccoli, trimmed and cut into small florets, with most of the stalks removed

½ cup fresh green peas

¾ cup young spinach or kale leaves, washed and roughly chopped (if using kale, be sure it is young and tender; otherwise, remove the tougher spines and discard)

1½ cups heavy cream

Salt, to taste

White pepper, to taste

Finely chopped fresh parsley, chives, and dill, for garnish

In a medium-size pot, cook the butter over medium heat until it begins to get foamy. Add the flour and whisk constantly, forming a roux. Cook until the roux is a deep, walnut brown and fragrant. Add 2 cups water and a pinch of salt, whisking until all lumps of the roux disappear.

Add the potatoes and simmer for 5 minutes. Add the carrots and continue to simmer for another 3 to 4 minutes before adding the onions and celery, then simmer for another 2 minutes. Timing here is approximate and dependent on the size of your vegetables.

Decrease the heat to medium low and add the milk. Check the doneness of your vegetables. The potatoes should be cooked through, while everything else should be partly cooked (think al dente pasta). Bring the mixture to a low simmer before adding the cauliflower, broccoli, peas, and leafy greens. Add a pinch of salt here as well. Simmer briefly, about 5 minutes or until all the vegetables are cooked through to your preferred level of doneness.

Add the cream and cook just enough to heat through, being careful not to bring the pot to a full boil. Add a pinch of salt and a little pepper (we prefer white pepper for this recipe). Taste and adjust the seasoning.

Serve in small, warmed bowls, ensuring that each guest gets a bit of each of the vegetables. Sprinkle a final pinch of salt and pepper over the bowls and garnish with chopped herbs.

DT SLOE

This was a drink created by one of our bartenders, Chris Buerkle, to play off the popularity of the Sloe Gin Fizz (see page 60). Chris absolutely loves rhum agricole, an exclusive product of Martinique and Guadeloupe. Most rums are made from various byproducts of sugar processing or molasses. However, with rhum agricole, which is a legally recognized category (much like champagne or cognac), fresh-cut sugarcane is immediately pressed, then fermented and distilled. The result is a very flavorful rum with grassy and herbal notes along with the traditional tropical fruit flavors you typically find in rum. Most often, rhum agricole is consumed unaged, though many producers lay some rum down in barrels for a special treat.

YIELD: 1 DRINK ⮞ **GLASS: CHILLED SINGLE OLD FASHIONED**

1½ ounces white rhum agricole (we use Clément Canne Bleue)

1 ounce sloe gin (use the best you can find; we use Plymouth's)

½ ounce fresh lime juice

½ ounce rich simple syrup (see page 191)

2 dashes Peychaud's bitters

Combine the rhum agricole, sloe gin, lime juice, syrup, and bitters in a mixing tin.

Fill with ice, cap the tin, and shake hard for 20 seconds.

Fine strain the drink into a chilled single old fashioned glass without ice. Drink quickly.

CHILTON COUNTY

In between living in Portland, Oregon, and Portland, Maine, we briefly lived in the Deep South—Alabama, to be exact. In our short time down there, we spent almost all of our free moments exploring the towns and beaches around us. On one particularly wonderful weekend, coming home from the Tennessee Valley, we stopped at a farm stand in Chilton County. This is where we discovered the best peaches in the world. No slight to Georgia, who I'm sure would disagree, but in our minds the best peaches are Alabama peaches. They are also what inspired this drink. Created in Mobile, Alabama, with those famous Chilton County peaches, this recipe makes us think of summer, driving around with no air conditioning, and fireflies. Sweet memories.

YIELD: 1 DRINK ✐ **GLASS: CHILLED DOUBLE OLD FASHIONED**

1½ ounces bourbon

¾ ounce fresh lemon juice

½ ounce rich simple syrup (see page 191)

1 teaspoon Peach Jam (recipe follows)

1 dash Angostura bitters

½ ounce egg white

Lemon peel and Angostura bitters, for garnish

Combine the bourbon, lemon juice, syrup, jam, bitters, and egg white in a mixing tin.

Fill the tin with ice, cap, and shake hard for 20 seconds.

Fine strain back into the mixing tin without ice. Cap and shake hard for 10 seconds to further emulsify.

Pour the drink into a chilled double old fashioned glass and add fresh ice. Garnish with a lemon peel and a dash of bitters.

PEACH JAM

YIELD: 4 CUPS (SAVE WHATEVER ISN'T USED IN COCKTAILS FOR TOAST THE NEXT MORNING)

12 ripe peaches

2 cups sugar, or to taste

½ teaspoon freshly grated nutmeg

Bring a large pot of water to boil. Get a large bowl filled with ice and water ready.

Score the bottom of each peach with an *X*. When the water is boiling, place 3 or 4 peaches into the water at a time (no need to crowd the pot) for 1 minute. After 1 minute, remove the peaches and immediately place them in the ice bath. Continue until all of the peaches are in the ice bath.

Once cool, peel each of the peaches and chop them into ½-inch pieces, removing and discarding the pits. Place the peaches, sugar, and 2 cups water into a pot over medium heat and bring to a simmer. Lower the heat to maintain a simmer and cook down until the mixture has thickened enough to coat the back of a spoon. Taste and adjust the sugar if needed.

Remove the mixture from the heat and stir in the nutmeg. Let cool and use immediately or keep in the refrigerator until ready to use. This will keep, refrigerated, for up to 1 month, but we hope it won't last that long. It also goes well on your morning toast.

GLOSSARY

ABV/PROOF: ABV (alcohol by volume) or proof is a standard unit of measure relating to how much alcohol is in a product as compared to its overall volume. In the United States, we have two measures: ABV is the mathematical amount of alcohol by volume (say 40 percent), while proof is a number that represents the same and is equal to twice the ABV. *Proof* dates back to the 1600s, before we were able to determine specific alcohol by volume measures. It has varied in its definition over the years. In our opinion, *proof*, though still legally printed on labels, is a bit of an outdated and confusing term. We stick to speaking about ABV of a spirit or cocktail.

AMARO/DIGESTIF: Amari (plural of amaro) and digestifs exist in a bit of a gray area between straight distilled liquor (think vodka, bourbon, and so on) and sweetened liqueurs (coffee, Irish cream, dry curaçao, and so on). They run the flavor range from bitter to bittersweet and can be low in proof (around 20% ABV) to just as strong as any liquor (40% ABV and higher). Amari and digestifs come from the European tradition of drinks that aid in the digestion of meals. They are often sipped in small quantities alongside shots of espresso in the afternoon or poured as rounds to savor and relax with after a multicourse feast. They have found new life in the cocktail world, both on their own and as components bringing complex flavors and layers to cocktails. There isn't necessarily a strong defining line between these categories and some liqueurs or aperitifs (which "open" the appetite before a meal), and while *amaro* specifically refers to a liquid poured from a single bottle, *digestif* can refer not just to a single pour but also to a cocktail made to aid in digestion (the Smoke + Bitters on page 42 works marvelously after a meal).

ATOMIZER: An atomizer is a small misting bottle with a pump top. It's used to impart the aroma but not the flavor of an ingredient in a drink. Behind the bar at Hunt + Alpine, we keep strongly flavored ingredients (such as Islay Scotch and absinthe) in atomizers and use two or three pumps to top a drink or line a glass with the slightest hint of these ingredients. This is used in place of rinsing a glass, which we feel can leave too much of an ingredient in the glass.

BATCHING: This is the process of preparing large amounts of a drink before a party or group arrives.

BITTERS: Bitters are alcoholic infusions or distillates with a bitter profile. Some are intended to be non-potable and added by the drop or dash (Angostura and Peychaud's), while others are drinkable on their own (like amari). Generally when we discuss using bitters in cocktails, we equate it to using salt in cooking. Bitters often bind flavors together or highlight certain elements. They're used in small doses, and when used correctly, they often don't stand out in the drink but instead make the other ingredients look good.

FINE STRAIN: Also known as double straining, fine straining removes tiny ice shards from a drink after shaking it vigorously in a mixing tin. We use both a Hawthorne strainer and a fine tea strainer to achieve a silky-smooth texture on shaken drinks, especially those made with egg whites.

SALINE SOLUTION: Just like in cooking, a small amount of salt can truly elevate flavors in a cocktail. To use salt, occasionally we'll pinch some kosher salt into a drink, but we also keep a small dropper bottle filled with a saline solution to ensure consistency in preparation of our drinks. This solution is made by mixing four parts warm water with one part kosher salt and stirring until the salt is totally dissolved. Funnel that into a dropper bottle and keep it near your bitters. It won't go bad, and it can truly make the difference in a cocktail.

RICH SIMPLE SYRUP: We use a thicker sugar syrup than the standard simple syrup (which is made with one part sugar and one part water) at Hunt + Alpine. Our syrup is made with two parts sugar to one part hot water, by weight instead of volume. Using a kitchen scale is the only way you will ensure consistency throughout your drinks and the recipes within this book. Once mixed, we continue to agitate the syrup until the sugar is completely dissolved into the solution. Using this allows us to easily provide a slightly thicker texture to a drink by adding the same amount of sugar with less water added. It is an easy-to-make and versatile syrup that we keep on hand both at Hunt + Alpine and in our refrigerator. There are plenty of paths to explore—using different types of sugar, flavoring the syrup, or implementing thickening agents to the syrup—but we continually come back to this simple, accessible, and versatile iteration.

THANK YOU

Our biggest thanks go to Oona and Rockwell, our sweet children, who have known nothing else but restaurants and bars their whole little lives. They are patient, kind, smart, and great eaters. Everything we do is for you two. This book is for you.

Our parents (Bee and Dave, Mary and Tim), our grandparents (Ray and Verna, Eda and John, Pam), and our siblings (Emma, Than, and Deems).

Trey Hughes, our bar manager at Hunt + Alpine. You are crazy talented, hard working, and so damn nice. None of this would be as great without you. Thanks for taking a chance with us and being here since day one.

And everyone who has ever worked for us: you all have believed in our vision and helped make it even better than we could have dreamed. Chefs Ricky, Stan, and Cory have made us more than a cocktail bar by making our food as good as our drinks.

Clyde Common, but mostly Nate Tilden and Jeffrey Morgenthaler. Thanks for being the reason we met, the place we got engaged, and an inspiration to us. Thank you for being sounding boards when we have no idea what we're doing, sharing great meals with us, and leading our industry by example.

Elisa, we just love you a lot. Thanks for sharing meals, drinks, houses in Palm Springs, and your love with us.

Thom O'Hearn, our editor. Thank you for giving us this opportunity and being super patient as we wrote this book (while opening another business and having a baby). Thank you for believing in us, this book, and our vision . . . and thanks for not yelling at us when we missed ~~almost~~ every deadline. Peter Frank Edwards and Sandy Lang, thank you for ensuring each and every photo in this book brought our vision to life.

And to the very early supporters of Hunt + Alpine who believed in our vision before our doors even opened: Brenda Garrand, Tay Veitch, Peter Richardson, Sam Beal, Bill Pusey, Brian Eng, Michael Lunn, Adam Nappi, Mark & Julie Basol, John Hatzenbuehler, Ben Jenkinson, Chris Marzzurco, Jed Harris, Drew Swenson, Anne Verrill, Jim Brady, Matt Schumacher, John Rogers, Maggie Knowles, Nick Dambrie. Especially Ian Malin, for his trust and generous support from the beginning and to this day.

ABOUT THE AUTHORS

Andrew Volk has been bartending for more than 15 years, working at some of the country's best bars. In 2013, Andrew and his wife Briana opened the Portland Hunt + Alpine Club, a cocktail bar with good drinks and Scandinavian-inspired food. Since opening, the bar has twice been named a James Beard Foundation semi-finalist for "Outstanding Bar Program" and was named by *Bon Appétit* as one of the "5 Best New Cocktail Bars in America." Andrew was named by *Food & Wine* as one of its 2016 "Best New Mixologists." His recipes have been featured by *Bon Appétit*, *Food & Wine*, *Maxim*, *Imbibe*, *Elle Décor*, the *Washington Post*, *NPR*, and more.

Briana Volk is a writer/creative director who worked in advertising, TV, and film before opening Hunt + Alpine with Andrew. She was the founding vice president of the Maine chapter of the United States Bartenders' Guild and founder of the New England Cocktail Conference. Since opening Hunt + Alpine, Briana has traveled the country speaking at conferences on bar and restaurant branding and design. As the creative director of both Hunt + Alpine and their second restaurant, Little Giant, Briana oversees the restaurants' look and feel, as well as their overall interiors. Her Finnish heritage influenced the menu at Hunt + Alpine, pulling from recipes and stories passed down through her family.

They live in Portland, Maine, with their two children, Oona and Rockwell.

INDEX

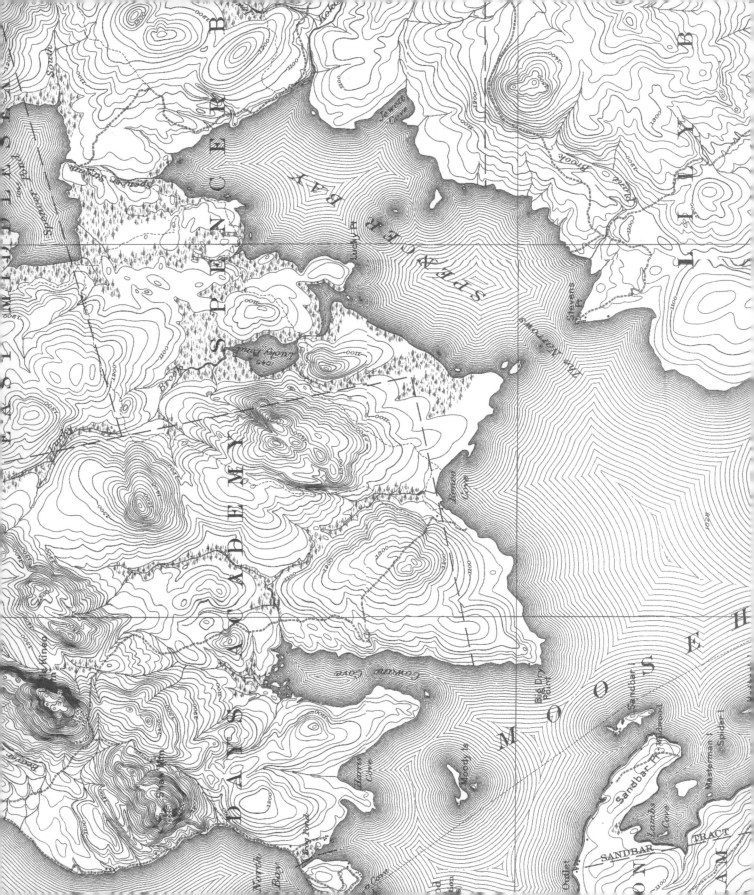